Born and brought up in New Delhi, **Sakshi Salve** holds a bachelor's degree in business management from the University of Exeter, UK. After working for one year at a reputed fashion house in London, she had two stints in the banking sector at UBS and Barclays, following which she moved back to New Delhi to set up a lifestyle store at the DLF Emporio mall with her mother. Her love for fine dining took her back to London, where she completed a comprehensive culinary course from the reputed Le Cordon Bleu. She also spent a summer in New York City and completed an intense scriptwriting course from New York University.

Sakshi loves to travel, is a voracious reader and is instinctively drawn to all things spiritual. She divides her time between New Delhi and London, and is now planning to pursue full-time writing and entertainment.

The Big
Indian
Wedding
The Ultimate Guide
For Dummies

Sakshi Salve

RUPA

Sales Centres:

Allahabad Bengaluru Chennai
Hyderabad Jaipur Kathmandu
Kolkata Mumbai

ISBN: 978-81-291-3744-9

Second impression 2015

10 9 8 7 6 5 4 3 2

The moral right of the author has been asserted.

Printed by HT Media Ltd., Noida

To my dearest (late) Phiroz Uncle

You loved us dearly and left us suddenly, but there is
not a moment when we don't feel your love around us.
Your irrepressible wit left an indelible impression — of
which you will find evidence in the following pages.

Contents

Foreword

The irony is that both the author, Sakshi Salve and I, are unmarried. I don't know her reasons for not embracing this rather quirky world of relationships mired initially in commerce, but mine are pretty simple. I don't want to marry only because I don't want a wedding. But then these are tough times for such demands. Everyone wants a wedding just like in yesteryears everyone loved a drought.

A wedding is a tedious event. It drives almost all involved in it, insane. I can take a wager that more divorces are planned during the wedding than after. The groom and the bride see the real colours of the families they are about to inherit—louts drinking whisky; then getting the horse to drink it; and then finally, getting the priest stoned only so that he can rush the actual ceremony so that they can go back to drinking. More Indians are drunk at their own weddings than any other race on this planet. More food is eaten during an Indian wedding than all the combined years of Taste of London. More Indian designers can still call themselves that because just being a wedding tailor is not enough.

I have seen more ugly people at Indian weddings than even in India's Parliament. But then that is not where it stops. The Indian wedding is not intended to be pleasant. Everything reeks of violence. You slap your in-laws on their backs, then you lift them, then you drop them to the ground; you then hide the shoes of that sod of a groom and then you run after them; then you encourage incest amongst cousins; and then everyone is happily drunk only to wake up the following day to get drunk again.

Then, of course, there is the small matter of the family. You will have relatives coming out of the woodwork and each of these dolts has to be sent an expensive wedding card: one card could feed a hundred Somalian pirates for a month, but then, who cares?

And our weddings are no longer confined to the family. You must invite the local lout (read: minister). You must have at least seven functions; you must engage a wedding planner and most of them are brain dead, which is why now even some fashion designers are quickly getting onto the wedding bandwagon. You must invite those people who you need to curry favour with—which means anyone from the local excise inspector to the local bootlegger. Then there are the Bollywood stars you can rent. If you pay them more, they will dance with the horse; if you pay then even more, they will be willing to allow you to ride them or at least some delicious cousin of yours who is not married yet.

But again the nuptials are the least important. You will need to plan the entertainment as well—and, at times, the entertainment and not the silly couple is the real draw. I mean, if you told me Jennifer Lopez would sing and then take her clothes off, do you really think I would bother with the names of those getting married?

You will also see the ubiquitous VIP corner in most Indian weddings. If the wedding is in Delhi, it will be meant for the prime minister who may not have been invited—but then, it's the effect. If it's Mumbai, then probably you can expect Salman Khan and if you are really desperate you might even settle for Raj Thackeray.

The Indian wedding is everything other than the wedding. Those who gush about the event and are found at each one of these are like the jokers who prefer an airline lounge to the actual journey itself.

I have rarely attended Indian weddings. I prefer funerals. I have seen with acute anguish how some Indians have managed to ruin fine European cities with their brand of the Indian wedding. Venice weeps while Paris perishes. Istanbul is so deeply disturbed that even its politics have begun to resemble the Indian wedding—all sound and even greater fury.

I have seen families embrace penury at the wedding altar. I have seen families climb onto rich lists thanks to weddings. I have seen more balance sheets being exchanged at weddings than gifts and more gold than what's available at Fort Knox. I have seen more people struggling to recognize the host or the bride and groom than trying to find sanity in Arvind Kejriwal.

Which is why Sakshi Salve's book is compelling and delightful. She weaves a tapestry of divine human proportions—from the influences that Bollywood may have had on the quintessential Indian wedding to the crassness, which is almost always on display. Sakshi evocatively puts forth both the plight and passion of the Indian wedding. And in doing so, she opens a wonderful world of which even though we may have been part, we never stopped to ponder over or stooped to conquer.

Sakshi Salve eloquently captures the evolution of the Indian wedding—from ceremony then to event now. She deftly tells a tale of greed and avarice, which have replaced the sanctity of hymns and harmony. The bondage of yore was between wife and husband. Today it is the bondage to materialism and commerce that almost always win a march. In doing so, Sakshi allows the reader to get a peep into the sociological impact of the Indian wedding—on emotions and economy alike.

Many films have been made around the Indian wedding. Songs have been sung and item numbers have been created. Odes and audaciousness apart, the spectacle of the Indian wedding almost always provokes curiosity, if not derision. A book like the one Sakshi has written further offers insights into not just the Indian wedding, but us as a people—an effort which is both laudable and timely.

This is a fine book about the infinite virtues of the modern Indian wedding. It will make you laugh; it will make you reflect; it will perhaps make you introspect; and for all we know even help you prepare for your version of the Indian wedding. Enjoy it as I set out to shred the next wedding invitation from people I have never known.

Suhel Seth
London, 2015

The Big Indian Wedding: The Boom and the Four-lettered Word

Remember the good old days? There were no cell phones; people drove around in Ambassador cars; girls from good families didn't stay out after dark and most marriages were 'arranged'. Big Indian weddings were more of a transaction rather than a bond of love, based on the economic and social standing of the families. Girls were married off into good 'khaandaani' households (read as loaded families), and the boys' parents wanted a typical 'sunder' and 'susheel' bahu (in short SUSU), a perfect domesticated homemaker, who would run the house and have lots of babies. The women sat at home, even if they

1

had valid degrees because *nahi toh, khaana kaun banayega?* If the bride saw the groom right before the wedding, it was considered inauspicious. In fact, it was quite common for them to not meet at all, until the day of the wedding itself.

Now, we are not a backward, illiterate third world country, where we blindly follow these dumb rules. There was good reason, or at least some reason, for this outdated tradition. A smooth wedding ceremony was ensured, as neither the bride nor groom had a clue as to who they were marrying—so no chance of dispute. It was a merger between two families. The boy and girl had no choice but to fall in love with each other—or at least, pretend to be in love. No one ever addressed the 'elephant' in the room, as denial was the norm back then. Girls were brainwashed and conditioned to please their husbands and in-laws, no matter what, and firmly warned that they could leave the husband's house only once they were dead.

Cut to the present day, where we are completely aping the West, with dating, mating and one-night stands. The concept of 'happily ever after' mostly exists in fairy tales and rom-coms. The sacred festival of karva chauth takes place on Facebook and Instagram and youngsters are no longer scared of their parents, choosing fun over fear. These days, it's very normal for a couple to be in a liquor-induced somnolent state throughout most of their dating period. Even wedding vows are taken while both the bride and groom are seriously hungover, undernourished, sleep-deprived and socially maxed out. It's interesting how one is expected to lunge into the sacred bonds of matrimony while trying to stay awake and refrain from throwing up. Then again, some things have not changed all that much. It's the modern-day illusion of a love marriage, when in reality, most of these 'love marriages' are essentially arranged. The only difference is that in the olden days, parents played a dominant role in introducing the boy and girl, now it's mostly Café Patron. No disrespect to other spirits such as beer, wine, whisky and vodka, but based on my personal observations and experiences, there is no greater cupid than tequila with a dash of caffeine!

Going back decades, most of the wedding work was delegated to family members and close friends, who came together to plan, organize and celebrate the special occasion. Several pujas and havans (religious offerings) created the pre-wedding build-up and excitement to bless the couple and pray for their future happiness.

This is an interesting contrast to current times, where pujas have been replaced by parties and Bloody Marys play a vital role in the couples' future happiness. Only the wedding planners know what the hell is going on. The bride and groom are excused from the extensive wedding planning exercises, as they have better things to do like shopping and planning holidays. The wedding planning team is paid a lot of money to substitute for friends and family. Everyone wants their daughter's or son's wedding to be better than 'his' daughter's and 'her' son's. Wedding coordinators are more like spies sharing their previous experience with clients and helping them top the last wedding. The Indian wedding has transformed into societal competition, with lavish displays of wealth, grandeur and an exaggerated notion of status. The union of two human beings has merely turned into a peg on which to hang the social extravaganza that we call a wedding.

I am not here to judge. I am merely an observer. I do not mean to be biased or offend anyone. A wedding is very personal and families are free to choose how they want to celebrate this so-called once-in-a-lifetime occasion. The fact that there has been a 100 per cent increase in divorce rates, and the chance of newlyweds staying together for the rest of their lives are slimmer than ever is a whole new topic that I am reserving for my next book!

Before we start this journey that encompasses the entire shebang associated with the magnificent affair, starting from the proposal all the way to the honeymoon, let's have a look at some basic statistics and facts. Ten million Indian weddings take place every year with approximately 30,000 weddings every day. The wedding industry is estimated to be worth a staggering US$38 billion and growing at the explosive rate of 25 to 30 per cent every year.[1] Even during recession, this industry stood at a huge figure of US$25 billion.

The creation of overnight fortunes due to speedy economic growth in India is responsible for creating a conspicuous, yet almost desperate type of consumption at weddings. The average middle-class budget for an Indian wedding is estimated to be around US$34,000 (around ₹19.01 lakh). The upper-middle and rich classes are estimated to spend upward of US$1 million (₹5.59 crore).[2] This doesn't include cash and valuables given as part of the gift exchange.

A typical Indian wedding in the US costs between US$75,000 and US$100,000—three times more than the average American nuptials.[3] Just imagine the opulence of

---

1. 'Inside India's Big Fat $38 Billion Wedding Market', *Business of Fashion*, in <http://www.businessoffashion.com/articles/global-currents/inside-indias-big-fat-38-billion-wedding-market-part-1-rohit-bal-sabyasachi-mukherjee-alex-kuruvilla-vijay-singh-india-bridal-fashion-week>, 7 August 2013, accessed on 18 June 2015.
2. 'The Indian Wedding Gets Fatter', *Hindustan Times*, in <http://www.hindustantimes.com/brunch/brunch-stories/the-indian-wedding-gets-fatter/article1-901951.aspx#sthash.VLaSrG9U.dpuf>, 29 June 2012, accessed on 18 June 2015.
3. 'Exclusively.In Targets $20 Billion Indian Wedding Market with New Online Boutique', *Forbes.com*, in <http://www.forbes.com/sites/lydiadishman/2011/05/13/exclusively-in-targets-200b-indian-wedding-market-with-new-online-boutique/>, 13 May 2011, accessed on 18 June 2015.

an Indian wedding—silk embroidered saris and lehengas, adorned with tonnes of Swarovski and countless semi-precious stones; precious gem-encrusted jewellery; a riot of flowers and enough food and drink to feed a small town. In addition to these basic requirements, a huge amount of money is lavishly spent on decorations, processions, band sets, video shooting, music, orchestra, film stars, exotic locations and so on.

The sheer scale of jewellery at high-end Indian weddings is mindboggling, with an overall budget of about US$500,000 spent on jewellery alone for the bride. Likewise, the clothing budget can easily surpass US$500,000, with scores of people to dress from the families. The annual worth of the wedding invitation card market is ₹10,000 crore—anything between ₹500 to ₹5,000 per card. No Indian bride is complete without the evergreen traditional bridal mehndi, again a ₹5,000-crore industry.

Bridal make-up is not what it used to be. These days brides want to look like Katrina Kaif and Kareena Kapoor—making this, once again, a booming industry, where a bride is charged anything between ₹20,000 (US$350) to ₹5,00,000 (US$8,500), depending on the make-up artist.

The two major hot spots for destination weddings in India are Rajasthan and Goa, where the cost of weddings is anywhere between a minimum of ₹1,00,00,000 to ₹2,00,00,000. As the Indian wedding market is getting bigger and bigger, basic pandal and decoration choices have been replaced by flashier décor. Farmhouses, hotels and palaces have replaced the home as venues, providing a completely new platform for decorators and wedding planners.

Even wedding cuisines are no longer the same, as everyone wants something different. So apart from typical Indian regional cuisines, others such as Continental, Lebanese, Thai, Chinese, Japanese and Italian are in high demand for marriages these days.

With an increase in the couples' demands and a search for exotic and romantic spots not just for their honeymoon, but also for proposals and destination weddings, the wedding business is spiralling into travel and tourism.

There are around 2,000 high-end weddings in India, annually. These are multi-day extravaganzas, complete with pyrotechnics, performances by Bollywood actors, international music stars and thousands of invited guests. Each year, these weddings manage to reach new heights, as prominent families aim to outdo each other with bigger events and newer, more exotic destinations, overelaborate parties for youngsters, bachelors and bachelorettes and last but not the least, expensive clothes and fine jewellery.

For India's ultra-high-net-worth individuals, it seems no gift is too lavish and no event is too opulent during the wedding season. Budgets for a high-end Indian wedding can easily reach up to US$2 million, including the cost of events, travel, food, clothing and especially, jewellery. Much of this money is spent in cash, as people have so much undeclared wealth—this is clearly the best way to spend it!

There is no doubt that Indian weddings are by far the most lavish, decadent and fun. No other country in the world can boast of their weddings the way we do. We may not have the best infrastructure and our hygiene levels are frighteningly low, but when it comes to any kind of celebration, especially weddings—we Indians kick ass!

So let's take a sneak peek into the world of the Big Fat Indian Wedding with all its drama, excitement and glory!

The Proposal: Size Does Matter

Historically, there were no proposals between the boy and girl. Proposals took place between two families over garam-garam chai, sweet-sweet ladoos and lots of pakodas and samosas. The demure bride-to-be would serve the hot tea and mouth-watering (artery-clogging) snacks, dressed up in her grandmother's heaviest brocade sari, probably loaded with the same jewellery that her mother wore for her wedding. I guess the saying, *'Jo dikhta hai woh biktaa hai'* is somewhat true. Once the families were satisfied with one another's wealth assessment, the liberal families sent off the boy and girl to have the most awkward private ten-minute conversation of their lives, while being stared at by the rest of the family. For the conservative ones, even this little indulgence was frowned upon.

It was all very simple. The boy's parents wanted a daughter-in-law who would cook, clean, sew and bear many children. The girl's parents wanted a son-in-law from a well-respected rich family, where their daughter could enjoy all the material happiness that money could buy—while chopping onions, of course.

These days proposals have escalated to a whole new level. London, Capri, Paris, Santorini, Maldives, just to name a few of the ever-growing exotic spots for the modern-day proposal.

What's the modern-day proposal, you ask? Let me explain. 'If so-and-so was taken to Italy, then why did my fiancé propose to me in Hyde Park? Oh wait, Hyde Park would have been fine if I didn't live in London, but since I do, proposing in a local venue is as good as "proposal suicide"!' Creativity and showmanship have replaced genuine heartfelt emotions and there is a greater emphasis placed on labels, rather than on love. There was a time when young girls would dream of their ideal man; these days they are obsessed with their dream proposal. I didn't make the rules but can safely say that the perfect proposal has to fulfil the following criteria—it has to be done somewhere 'abroad'; it has to involve a five-carat ring, a private jet or yacht, minimum ten gallons of champagne, and a view of the ocean. And that, my friends, is the definition of the modern-day proposal.

It's very interesting how the entire world of wedding proposals has reached new levels of imagination and expenditure. A decade ago, a plain simple 'will you marry me?' at the couples' favourite restaurant with the guy on his knees (even figuratively) would be enough to make the girl go weak in her knees. But this trend is completely out of fashion now, just like the leopard print. So what is in fashion these days? Let's have a look.

The Karan Johar Proposal

When it comes to Karan Johar's movies, whether it's *Kuch Kuch Hota Hai*, *Student of the Year* or *Yeh Jawaani Hai Deewani*, our modern-day love-guru knows exactly how to market the concept of love and romance—casting a magical spell on his audience and making them want to fall in love instantly.

The Karan Johar Proposal stands for lots of red and bling. Red roses, red carpet, red cake, red candles, and if diamonds were red, then maybe even a red ring. My sister experienced this kind of very filmy proposal on Valentine's Day itself! A royal red carpet welcome with a stunning gazebo decorated with chandeliers, hanging crystals and pearls, shiny disco balls and psychedelic waterfalls.

Excitement started from noon onwards, when she started receiving flowers and gifts by the hour, every hour—building up to the 'ishq wala love' proposal. The same evening, when she walked into her (at the time) boyfriend's house in her sexy red dress, she was absolutely floored by his efforts to make the place look like a movie set waiting to shoot a proposal scene. Imagine a gigantic bouquet of a thousand roses, a long-stemmed stand-alone rose, and the engagement ring concealed in the midst of its petals. Which girl would not feel like a movie star and be swept off her feet?

Candles lit up the entire venue, highlighting the thousand-rose bouquet, the heart-shaped balloons, a red heart-shaped cake, red carnations and roses, and most importantly, a colossal amount of champagne. A tall, dark and handsome man in his tux and red tie was waiting to go down on his knees. My now brother-in-law had left no stone unturned! It's almost as if he had a checklist from Karan Johar's production team. It's funny how when we see this same stuff in movies, we laugh and call it cheesy. But deep down, every girl secretly wants to be wooed in proper fairy tale Bollywood style. (Okay, I don't know about *every* girl, but I definitely do!)

The Sanjay Leela Bhansali Proposal

When Sanjay Leela Bhansali sets out to make a film, one thing that's guaranteed is the magnificence and opulence attached to everything he does. Every frame is a work of art—and everything from the characters to the costumes to the music and drama is well researched and full of colour and life. He is an ardent follower of customs and traditions, which are reflected in his films. As the founder of larger-than-life cinema, it is no surprise that this old-school love-guru inspires young men these days.

The main prerequisite for a Sanjay Leela Bhansali Proposal is going back in time to an entirely different era, a different world. Despite our lives being dominated by technology these days, when it comes to matters of the heart, old is definitely gold. I know of someone who re-created such old-world charm at the world's most romantic Taj Lake Palace Hotel in Udaipur. Imagine this most stunning palatial structure, surrounded by clear emerald green water, with the rays of the setting sun making the lake shimmer like diamonds. The lovebirds were nestled in a boat filled with the most decadent chocolates, the most expensive flowers money can buy, the best champagne known to man, and of course, lots of love. The big rock was cleverly hidden in an ice cube and casually dropped into one of the champagne glasses.

The smallest detail of this regal proposal was looked into, including an orchestra playing romantic tunes for the couple right in the middle of the lake. If this is not the stuff movies are made of, then I don't know what is.

Our man of the moment (the proposer) could have gone the Karan Johar way, but decided to stick to an old-school expression of love. It's a different matter that I don't understand how this is old school, because back in the day, people neither had the funds nor the brains to come up with something even remotely similar. But these days, being transported back a generation or two requires little imagination and lots of cash. It's hard to tell if movies are inspired by reality or the other way round.

The Yash Raj Proposal

Yash Raj Films is probably one of the oldest and most popular schools of filmmaking. Getting into college is impossible without completing high school. Likewise, getting anywhere in Bollywood is next to impossible without passing the Yash Raj test. From *DDLJ* (*Dilwale Dulhania Le Jayenge*) to *Dhoom 3*, the films never fail to deliver the most exotic locations, erotic heroines (with family values), trendiest outfits, eight packs and *bahut saara pyaar*. The creator of Simran and Raj (our evergreen *pyaar ka baadshah*) Yash Raj's films are as dreamy as dreamy can get. It's hard to imagine a Yash Chopra film without an exotic location abroad.

Now, our final proposal story for you fits this mould perfectly. Our Romeo from New Delhi took his Juliet to the proposal capital—Capri—under the pretext of a holiday. Our *Dilli ka dilwaala* had cleverly conjured up a series of special moments, which would all lead up to the ultimate fairy tale proposal for his *Dilli ki billi*. A series of personally delivered calligraphic, handwritten cards by an unknown 'Mr X', acted as excellent props for a series of special events.

Day 1: The lovebirds are ready to rock (pun intended). The first day goes pretty much as the beginning of any other holiday, with plenty of eat, sleep, rave and repeat!

Day 2: With the first rays of the rising sun, the *pehle pyaar ki pehli chithhi* arrives from the mysterious 'Mr X', requesting our lady love to go and shop until she drops! Ooh la la...VIP...VIP...VIP all the way! That's how we Delhiites roll! Moving on, the same evening, another letter awaited our naughty billi, with detailed instructions to pamper herself at the spa, followed by a super-romantic evening under the stars.

Day 3: The D-day! *Dil bole haddipah! Yash Raj Proposal hai bhai, hero heroine ko character mein toh laana padega* (it's a Yash Raj Proposal after all; the boy and girl have to be in character). Top stylists of Italy were called to groom our *shehzaadi* for the evening, all orchestrated by our most wanted prince. With the shopping, spa pampering and grooming out of the way, she was now officially ready to be swept off her feet. There was yet another letter from 'Mr X', inviting both of them to a romantic candlelit dinner.

Just try to picture this: Capri, a sea of emotions and a million charming secrets to discover. Sitting perched high up on the cliff-face overlooking the waters, with a private chef, an uninterrupted view and no other tables in sight, our love-struck couple dined on the finest food Capri had to offer. Our prince, nervous like a little kitten, made many heartbeats skip by just looking at this stunning goddess sitting opposite him. They both pinched themselves, just to make sure that this was not a dream.

Our man himself presented the final envelope, where he revealed the mystery behind 'Mr X', got down on one knee and asked that ever-important question, 'Will you marry me?'. Our shocked, elated, teary-eyed princess tightly hugged him and said *yes*!

At this point, all of you must be wondering: 'Where on earth are these men?' Well, sadly, most of these rare gems are already married. And the remaining ones have run off to Bangkok, choosing ladyboys over depleted bank accounts.

I am not sure exactly when the landscape of the proposal industry transformed, but I think it has been a gradual uphill climb over the last decade. Once upon a time, a bunch of roses was enough to woo a girl, and now it takes a bunch of cruises to even initiate the process. An engagement ring was the symbol of love and togetherness, and it didn't matter what size the diamond was. These days, it's almost embarrassing to present a symbol of love with a diamond that is less than five carats. And you do not want to start a new chapter in your life with a kanjoos, who can't even provide you with this *basic* requirement. Of what use is the deep passionate love you share, when it does not come with a five-carat diamond, right?

There seems to be a lot of speculation regarding the perfect ring size. Should one go for quality or quantity? The bigger, the better? Or less is more? Unfortunately, there is no right answer. I personally would love a D-colour, ten-carat ring that drops the pants off people. While my male friends would have nightmares at the thought of spending so much hard(ly)-earned money on a crystal of carbon put under pressure, the truth—to quote someone famous—is that diamonds are forever, unlike most marriages.

After a dreamy fairy tale proposal, what comes next? Now it's time to take off those beer goggles, and stare reality in the face. *Pehle mazza, phir sazza!*

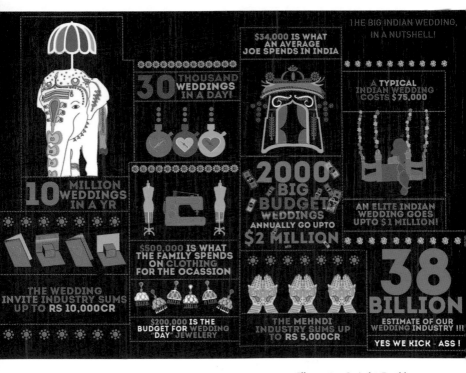

Illustration © Ankit Parikh

Illustration © Ankit Parikh

I love you, baby,
let's get wasted!
Modern love...

Starring Cafe Patron

we have so much in common!!

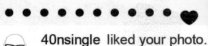

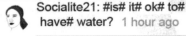

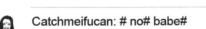

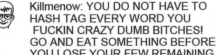

Illustration © Ankit Parikh

New age karva chauth on social media!

Illustration © Ankit Parikh

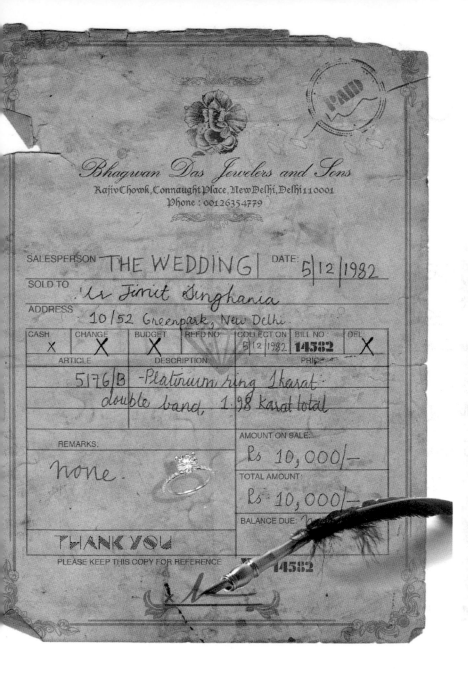

Bhagwan Das Jewelers and Sons

Rajiv Chowk, Connaught Place, New Delhi, Delhi 110001
Phone : 00126354779

| SALESPERSON | THE WEDDING | DATE: 5 | 12 | 1982 |

SOLD TO : Mr Jimit Singhania

ADDRESS : 10/52 Greenpark, New Delhi.

CASH	CHANGE	BUDGET	REFD NO	COLLECT ON	BILL NO	DEL
X	X	X		5 12 1982	14582	X

ARTICLE	DESCRIPTION	PRICE
5176/B	-Platinum ring 1 karat double band, 1.98 karat total	

REMARKS.

none.

AMOUNT ON SALE : Rs 10,000/-

TOTAL AMOUNT : Rs 10,000/-

BALANCE DUE :

THANK YOU

PLEASE KEEP THIS COPY FOR REFERENCE   14582

The world of Reciepts

arna Jewelers

Aarna Jewelers
South extention, Zafar nagar
Delhi- 110049
THIS SPACE FOR ADDRESS ONLY

Receipt

Made for Sameer Ahluwalia, the diamond is
5 karat cushion cut brilliant of VVSI clarity
of the color H certified duly by the
Gemological Institute of America also
holding IGI stamp.

Amount paid : 80 lakhs/—

X

Illustration © Ankit Parikh

Illustration © Ankit Parikh

Welcome to the Family:
The Titanic Test

*N*ow that you're hooked and booked, it's time to get cooked! Dating is a cakewalk compared to getting married. Once the proposal is out of the way, enter family and exit fun, romance and partying. Things suddenly escalate from neutral to fifth gear, making the couple wonder what the hell just happened. While dating, parents are people you say 'hi' or 'bye' to, either while entering or leaving your girlfriend/boyfriend's house. After the proposal, they become a big part of your life with at least 40 per cent of your plans revolving around them.

There has been an enormous progression from the past, when there was hardly any fun, romance or partying to begin with. Back in the day, girls were not allowed to stay out of the house beyond 10 p.m. (these were the liberal families) and marriage was their licence to freedom. No such thing as a girlfriend or a boyfriend existed and even if they did, the matter was kept a top secret. The previous generations believed in the sanctity of marriage and Sooraj Barjatya's hit movie plot—*ek ladka aur ladki kabhi dost nahi ho sakte* (a girl and boy can never be friends). It was either marriage or nothing.

My mother was introduced to my father when she was twenty-one, and three months later, they got married. That's how things were done back then. In fact, three months was considered too long a courtship period, with parents worried about familiarity breeding contempt. My mother fell in love with my father much later, I think around the time I was born—but she married him because since childhood, she was told that she could do whatever her heart desired after marriage. Whether it was a late night movie, a party or wearing a dress, the answer was, '*Beta, shaadi ke baad karna.*'

Marriage was the prize you won after years of following your father's orders and living by his rules. Blinded by the promise of the sweet nectar called freedom, girls were happy to oblige their in-laws—spend time with them, go shopping together, learn recipes from the mom-in-law—and let their lives revolve around their husbands (seems to me like 'free-dumb'). Hard to believe someone would do all this, for the occasional late night film or a glass of wine with dinner. It really was a simple time.

Fast forward thirty years and the father of the bride-to-be is relieved that now someone else will be paying all her bills, while the father of the groom-to-be is dealing with high blood pressure caused by unforeseen future expenditure. The bride-to-be is freaking out at the thought of not living with Mummy and Papa anymore. And the poor groom-to-be is trying to steer clear of a psycho mom-in-law, who basically wants to feed him until he dies.

Unlike the West, getting married in India means being married not just to your spouse, but the entire family, including the kutta, billi, Ramu and Shamu. Super-fun weekends with the boyfriend/girlfriend turn into super-long and super-tedious weekends with the to-be in-laws and their entire entourage of mamas, chachas, buas, masis, cousins and their annoying little kids. Hungover Sundays in bed become a distant memory, replaced by mind-numbing family lunches with irritating kids, who need to be taken to the toilet every ten minutes. These experiences make you want to be eaten alive by bees rather than get subjected to this weekly torture before (and after) marriage.

Every single uncle and aunt (even those you don't know) wants to know when he or she can have a party for you. These parties are basically for the boy's parents to flaunt their new daughter-in-law to be. And the girl's parents want to exhibit their future son-in-law to all their friends and family, especially those with unmarried daughters! Cruel is how we Indians like it! I remember my mother's proud grin while she introduced my brother-in-law (at the time of their wedding) to all the guests. She took personal credit for all his attributes—from his height to strength to brains—and was thrilled at the fact that this perfect boy was marrying her perfect daughter.

To make matters more interesting, all the single girls at these functions are asked the most outdated question, 'Beta, now it's your turn—when are you giving us the good news?' I mean, show some sensitivity, for god's sake. When we meet you at a funeral, do we say, 'Aunty, now it's your turn!'? Personally, when I am subjected to this kind of nonsense, my reply is, 'Going to London next month, will check out the "groom" section at Harrods!' Of course, this doesn't make me popular with the Delhi aunties, something I'm truly grateful for. A single guy, on the other hand, is never asked this question because '*arre, woh toh ladka hai, uski toh shaadi ho hi jayegi!*' It's this kind of mentality that boosts our country's progress. (Sarcasm alert!)

A very wise person once said, 'You don't know what you've got until it's gone!' Dating is truly the best time of anyone's life—with all the fun and none of the added liabilities. As if two parents weren't enough to suck the life out of you, now you have four. From '*ek main aur ek tu*' to '*hum saath saath hai*'. Oh lord, shoot me now!

↙

Now, let me explain the concept guiding the 'Titanic Test'. It's a cool quiz created by me to test your ability to withstand the sudden bombardment of attention and expectations from the 'new family'. I have prepared a few questions, and based on your answers, you will find out if:

a) You have the balls to create your own rules.
b) You're going to sink (just like the *Titanic*).
c) Diplomacy is your best friend.

The Titanic Test

1. How many late night Saturdays with friends have turned into Sunday brunches with the in-laws and extended family?
   a) Zero, actually.
   b) Every single weekend.
   c) Once in a while, it happens.

2. How many times a week are you expected to do the obligatory 'time-spend' with the in-laws?
    a) Once a month, if I feel like it.
    b) At least two or three times a week.
    c) Once a week.

3. How often have you had to lie to your mom-in-law and pretend you agree with her instead of voicing your own opinion?
    a) Never ever.
    b) Always but always.
    c) Now and again.

4. Have you ever lied to your partner in order to avoid a boring family commitment, and gone out with your friends instead?
    a) You bet! All the time!
    b) Are you kidding me? Of course not!
    c) Sometimes—we all need a break!

5. Can you get wasted in front of your in-laws?
    a) Hell, yeah!
    b) No frikkin' way, they don't even know I drink!
    c) A drink or two sometimes.

Congratulations! Now that you have embarked on this journey of self-discovery, read on for results! By the way, you have officially taken your first step towards letting me play with your minds. Just kidding, I am only trying to help!

Mostly a's — You know how to float your own boat

If your answers are mostly a's, then you are highly self-centred with balls of steel! You have clearly mastered the art of deception and you really don't give a rat's ass about anything! Ooohh, well done! People in this category often find themselves alone by mid-life, as they are not able to adapt or properly commit to anyone or anything. I recommend help! Maybe a trip to Bhutan to learn some humility from the monks.

Mostly b's — You're going down! Ouch!

If your answers are mostly b's, then you need more help than the a's. Sure b's are selfish and insensitive, but at least don't let people walk all over them! You guys need to grow a pair! Please stop being a doormat and stand up for yourself. The validation you crave from outside is already there within you. So stop being this perfect 'mannequin bahu' and/or 'trophy daamaad' and start believing in yourself! You can do it, just make a friend from the category above!

Mostly c's — You diplomatic shark!

If your answers are mostly c's, then why the hell are you wasting your time with this test! Instead, you should be running for president! You are the true rockstar, having mastered the art of keeping yourself and others happy. You fulfil your duties without being pushed around, maintaining a good equilibrium between your own desires as well as those of others. An inspiring example for today's youth, and our friends in the categories listed above! Bravo!

Disclaimer: I do not wish to offend. The test results help you understand yourselves better. Even if you are someone who cannot really change things, you don't need to worry. After all, you still have a bunch of super-entertaining chapters to read!

Enter Wedding Planner: Exit Bank Balance

In the good old days, wedding planners were unheard of, while these days a wedding without a planner is unheard of. Just as the fate of a film depends on the director, the fate of a wedding depends on the most 'in demand' wedding planner! Over the years, weddings have completely transformed in the upper echelons of society. Inspired by films like *Hum Aapke Hain Kaun*, families want a larger-than-life component in every aspect of a wedding—from the type of and number of functions, to a menu with multiple cuisines, a venue with a twist, professional entertainment and mindblowing décor.

When it comes to over-the-top weddings, money

27

is generally the last thing on Papa's mind. Whether it is spending on clothes, jewellery or the actual ceremonies, the affluent Indian will pull out the big guns—*kyunki rishtey mein toh hum tumhaare baap lagte hain*! In Delhi itself, the phrase 'big fat Indian wedding' is synonymous with the GDP of a small country. So yes, the Big Indian Wedding is no less than a multi-crore, multi-starrer, mega blockbuster.

North Indian weddings are not only serious business, but also sites of serious competition. Wedding planners use their creative skills, trusted professionals and reliable suppliers to transform any occasion to a uniquely signature event. The original task of understanding the couples' personalities, styles, likes and dislikes has now been replaced by a thorough understanding of parental insecurities due to societal pressure. Wedding planners are impressively clued in, and know exactly how to help parents win the wedding-competition. Gone are those days *jab baraatiyon ka swagat Pan Paraag se hota tha! Ab toh* vintage cars *ka zamaana hai* and the father of the bride *ko dulhe parr bahut saara paisa udaana hai!*

The success of a wedding is generally on account of a joint effort between wedding planners, lucky designers and the families of the bride and groom. Let's give you a step-by-step preview into the months of colossal effort that go into planning this multi-day extravaganza—which gets over in the blink of an eyelid.

Venue: Without a Venue, There Ain't No Wedding

Your wedding day supposedly comes once in a lifetime. No wonder people are going ape-shit willing to pay anything to make it unforgettable. It's not uncommon to hear a Dolly Aunty or a Sweety Uncle say, 'Kya *shaadi thi yaar, dil khush ho gaya.* They took us to Bali you know, *woh bhi* business class! And guess where we stayed? Four Seasons, yaar! All expenses paid of course! *Dekhna, mere Bunty ki shaadi bhi foreign mein hogi!* And everything seven star! Better than Pammi's daughters!'

The trend of celebrating Indian weddings at ancestral homes is now completely outdated, just as the old Windows PC is. The 'in' thing now is to either take your guests to an exotic holiday destination, or bring your holiday destination to your guests. It's mindboggling how spaces can be transformed to create the illusion of a destination wedding. A hotel ballroom can be redesigned as Bali, and a farmhouse can easily become Greece—all one needs is a BIG wedding planner and a BIGGER bank balance. Really, the different varieties of wedding venues available locally as well as internationally will shock you.

A destination wedding is a unique way of exchanging

vows, while surrounded with close friends and family. It allows you to filter out the crowd and call only those people who really matter. The fact that most Indian families have at least five hundred people in their 'have to invite' list is an entirely different matter! Destination weddings have greatly grown in popularity in recent years, with people very carefully selecting their perfect wedding venue, based on not only their tastes, but also the tastes and preferences of their hi-fi friends and family—*arre bhai, competition jeetna hai.*

For psychedelic beach party junkies, the obvious choice is Goa, with its exquisite mix of sun, surf and sand. Goa has become the ultimate wedding destination in India, because where else can the newly married couple hop from the sacred mandap straight to the full moon rave? And just like Vegas, whatever happens in Goa, stays in Goa!

If you are from the Sanjay Leela Bhansali school of thought, and belong to the BBC—the Blue Blooded Club, then the citadels of Rajasthan eagerly await you. Known as the city of lakes and palaces, Udaipur is really one of the most romantic and charming places in India. A lot of this charm comes from its regal architecture, with unique fairy-tale-like qualities. The pink city of Jaipur is also a favourite destination, with venues ranging from authentic, ornate palaces to old mansions to heritage venues away from the city. Then there's Jodhpur, with the extraordinary Umaid Bhawan Palace—with a hilltop location overlooking the blue city—playing host to some very lavish band-baaja-baraat weddings.

These are some of the favourite Indian destinations, but let's not forget some of the most desired international wedding locations—Mykonos, Bali and Istanbul, to name a few in the ever-growing list of spots for the Big Indian Wedding. Mehndi on a yacht, followed by champagne showers, and pheras by clear emerald green waters and sand like white talcum powder—what more can one ask for? Leading the list of foreign locales is Thailand—not only known for its happy endings and disturbed beginnings, but also popular for big Indian weddings. Recently added to this list are a few European cities such as Barcelona, Rome and, of course, the all-time favourite of the rich Indians—Paris!

Choosing the wedding venue is a royal pain in the ass, as everything is booked out at least a year in advance. Once the venue is booked, the wedding planners' rollercoaster begins! They have to make sure everything runs smoothly and coordinate all the different aspects that go hand-in-hand with making the wedding a memorable one!

Invites: This Ain't Just a Message No More

As autumn draws close, the social scene in the country rapidly accelerates. Come October, and it's time for the couture wedding invites to do the rounds. Gone are the days when a wedding invite was merely a formal message with dates, time and venues for the various functions that had to be attended. These days, wedding invites are as important as the wedding itself (with the 'dates' being imported from Dubai), reflecting the sender's bank balance and offering a sneak peak into what lies ahead. *Agar card mein nahi dum toh shaadi mein numbers honge kum!*

Now steps in a new trend of personalized, exquisite, out-of-the-box invites, with attention to the smallest details—the right font, specific colour combos and original designs, including an eclectic mix of astounding special 3-D effects! In fact, the contents of destination wedding invites include SIM cards, immigration forms, sunglasses for beach destinations, T-shirts and baggage tags—everything except the boarding pass!

These days, believe it or not, the latest 'in' thing is sending video invites! Clearly, Bollywood has had a huge impact, with people wanting to become literally the 'stars' of their wedding. So how does this work? It is simple. Guests receive either an iPad or a digital photo frame to plug in. Then the wedding promo starts with the bride and groom gazing into each other's eyes, both gleaming like glowworms, showing off their on-camera skills, while the wedding details (dates, time, venues) are melodramatically displayed in the background.

It's almost mandatory now to send an appropriate gift—or as we call it, 'shagun'—along with the invite. These gifts can range from a box of your yummy *motichoor ke ladoo*, to fancy silverware with expensive items like saffron, dry fruits, dates and silver-coated cardamom. Recently, bottles of vodka, Café Patron, whisky and so on have become popular add-ons to the fancy wedding invite—as a result of which, normal chocolates and mithai have become, like, *sooo* last season. *Arre bhai, Dolly Aunty ko bhi toh impress karna hai!*

The kind of things that one hears during this much-awaited season of the year is Oscar-winningly surreal! Our quintessential Dolly Aunty will say, '*Haii Ram! Aaj Dhingra ki beti ka wedding card aaya, by god, meri toh death hi ho gayi!* Each card must be at least two thou! *Agar invite aisa toh shaadi mein kitna kharcha karengey?*' And not to forget our favourite Sweety Uncle, a creature of humility (haha) and 130 kilos of pure fat, who will say things like, '*Oye Dolly, inka koi beta hai kya? Humaari Bubbli ke liye! Invite aisa hai toh ghar kaisa hoga!*'

I trust you are now up-to-date with the modern-day

concept of wedding invites, which have become status symbols, unlike in the past.

Food: Will the Real Foodies Please Stand Up?

There is a saying that goes something like—'Food is the way to a man's heart'. The truth? Food is the way to a man's heart attack! In today's day and age, the concept of fitness has been completely redefined and revolutionized to a whole new level. Women are back in the gym, literally weeks after giving birth, and men are waking up even before the milkman to get an hour of an intense workout before office. Gone are the days when love tyres were considered sexy and curves were considered cute. Six packs and size zeros are the new norm, again Bollywood zindabad! In this rat race for the perfect body, wedding time becomes an exception where everyone loses the plot! *Size zero ka zamaana hai, par shaadi pe sabko kutton ki taraah khaana hai!*

Apart from lavish décor and pimped out celebrations, Indian weddings are also known for their sumptuous lip-smacking food. In fact, weddings are incomplete without a grand feast guaranteed to put your guests into a food coma! Traditionally, it was customary to serve food specially made by a wedding-specialist cook or 'maharaj' (a common enough entity in affluent households). He would cook the food overnight in the backyard of the house, where the ground would be dug up for a wood fire; here, he'd keep churning out one dish after the other. Earlier, while cooks were hired for whipping up delicious dishes, nowadays most people opt for catering services with up to ten cuisines lined up. To win the wedding competition, you need to have at least ten varieties of starters, salads, curd, main course, and desserts from each cuisine. Anyone you have interacted with in your lifetime is fed until fed up. In fact, the current 'in' concept is to recreate spaces, like a Punjabi dhaba, a French café, a seafood shack and so on, so that the wedding guests feel like they've been transported to a holiday destination.

The pricing depends on the lavishness of the spread you choose—ranging from anywhere between ₹1,500 to ₹6,000 per plate, adding up to almost a third of the total wedding cost. We Indians will compromise on absolutely anything, but not food! Especially Dolly Aunty, who will fast two days before the mehndi because she wants to pig out on the chaat, chola baturas, pao bhaji, masala omelette and the colourful chuskis.

Unlike the mehndi ceremony, which consists mostly of chatpatta street food, the other wedding functions are known to offer every type of food available under the sun. The funniest thing is to watch the vegetarian aunties experiment with sushi, just to feel cool, even though they want to spit it out as soon as it touches their samosa-jalebi palates. The live pasta station and teppanyaki grills have lines longer than Space Mountain at Disney Land, as these dishes are perceived as being healthy yet yummy. *Figure bhi toh maintain karna hai!*

There is only one thing at a wedding function that's more important than food, and that's the booze.

Alcohol: Khaana Toh Kutte Khaate Hain! Insaan Sharaab Peetey Hain!

While the aunties are stuffing their faces, the uncles and youngsters are busy at the bar, oblivious to the concept of food. Traditionally, alcohol was a strict no at weddings, especially on the wedding day. Then the rules started changing and people started serving the good stuff, only closing the bar during the sacred pheras. From 'No Label' to 'Blue Label', now there are multiple bars at every wedding function, serving not only the best scotch and other hard liquor, but also the finest wines and champagne and a variety of chic cocktails out of *Sex and the City*. Bartenders are impressively trained to make cocktails that match people's outfits and moods. A good bartender is one who can just look at you and know what you want.

Another concept that has sky-rocketed over the last few years is that of shots! Shots are not what they once were, a tiny glass with either neat liquor or some kind of mixture that was gulped down in one go. Nowadays, we have shots in every colour, size and form imaginable. From test tube shots that are (obviously) served in test tubes, to injection shots in which the alcohol, in a syringe, is squirted into one's mouth, the whole agenda of drinking and getting drunk has evolved beyond comprehension. Once again, all thanks to Bollywood—*chaar bottle vodka... kaam mera roz ka!*

Once upon a time, a Hindi movie heroine was portrayed to be a sati-savitri, who would be horrified at the thought of her hero or her even having a sip of alcohol. It was meant to be evil, and only the villains had access to this forbidden nectar. Between the Gabbars and the Mogambos, our poor hero-heroine would be left with tears instead of beers. Thankfully, this school of thought is now outdated, with A-grade actresses being wasted on screen, enjoying champagne showers and wearing the latest and skimpiest outfits, giving their heroes a run for their money! Gone are the days when girls used to cook like their mothers—they now drink like their fathers! Someone wise once said: *Nasha agar sharaab mein hota toh naachtee bottle, nasha toh pilaane waalon ki aankhon mein hai!*

Hey Mr DJ: Sab ki Bajaate Raho!

From Chandni Chowk to Chinchpokli, no matter where you go, no party is complete without the most crucial ingredient—the DJ—who is responsible for making all your wedding functions rock. Unlike traditional weddings in the past—where a fat woman chewing tobacco, in a simple sari and with a big red bindi, was called to liven up the party with a mix of ghazals and Hindi movie songs—these days, a wedding function, big or small, is just not possible without the best DJ—not playing, but 'spinning' the coolest tracks and latest re-mixes, until the wee hours of the morning! Or shall we say, *jab tak Aunty police bulalegi?* Once drunk, the David Guettas and Aviciis of the world go right out the window, and the Bollywood in everyone comes oozing out, with a demand for Hindi songs hitting the roof. Even the judgemental aunties drop their guard and are seen doing the 'moves' in their backless cholis, creating tabaahi on the dance floor.

Over the years, the concept of 'partying' has done multiple somersaults—where once parties ended at 2 a.m., nowadays the 'real' party only begins at 3 a.m.! This creates another challenge for the DJs, who need to rock not just the parties, but the 'after parties' as well. In fact, at destination weddings, the after party is more important than the party itself, being the benchmark of a truly hit wedding!

Entertainment, Entertainment, Entertainment: The Soul of the Party

Just like my favourite movie, *The Dirty Picture*, weddings these days revolve around three things—entertainment, entertainment and more entertainment. Drinking, dining and dancing, the three Ds that are vital to the success of any party are not enough any more. Guests are not fully satisfied unless they have Yo Yo Honey Singh setting the stage on fire with his 'lungi dance', and Katrina Kaif fulfilling her duty by shaking that booty. People are going all out by spending massive amounts of money on not only Bollywood stars, but also international music artists, rappers, professional dancers, stand-up comedians and pretty much anything else or anyone who catches their fancy.

There's also a new fad—that of entertaining guests with fun videos of the couple; close family and friends tease the lovebirds, highlighting their romantic journey with humorous comments. In fact, my wedding gift to my sister was a very crazy over-the-top music video making fun of my sister's love for brands—starring the couple themselves, their close friends and me! *Jab wife ko pasand ho brands toh husband ka bajegaa band!*

Unbelievably, families and friends these days are under plenty of pressure to entertain wedding guests, along with the professional entertainers. It's almost a life and death competition between the girl's side and boy's side, with both parties trying to prove they are better entertainers. But more on this later, in a chapter dedicated to 'dance practice'—a major part of the pre-wedding preparations. The bride might forget the groom's name, but god forbid if the sangeet performance is not up to the mark—there will be consequences!

Speeches and toasts are prepared in advance, with plenty of practice and with the sole goal of entertainment. I myself have tweaked reality on many such occasions, after strict instructions from the couple as to what I can and cannot say. What couples need to understand is that it is very hard to say only nice things and make guests laugh at the same time! But what can I do?—couples these days are very demanding and won't take no for an answer; they want it all! *Jab dulha-dulhan fighter toh kya karega bechara writer!*

🌿

This wedding planning rollercoaster ride of venues, invites, food, alcohol, DJ and entertainment, as we now know, is all managed and coordinated by the wedding planner and a super-efficient team. Sometimes, I feel all the investment banking rejects get into this field for the big bucks and even bigger challenges, justifying their valuable degrees and hard work, while picking out carnations. So now, you know how important a good planner is, and how much stress they go through to make sure you have an unforgettable wedding.

I have only mentioned the main tasks that the planner is responsible for, but there are many other entities that his team must arrange for—dholwaalas, tentwaalas, lightwaalas, soundwaalas, choreographers, scriptwriters, mehndiwaalis, beauticians—the list is endless.

Retail Therapy:
Bridezilla Spends on Retail,
Groom on Therapy

A male friend of mine recently got married and the one complaint he had throughout was: 'What the fuck is wrong with women? The moment they are about to tie the knot, they start behaving like the world is ending and hence everything under the sun should be in their possession! I really do not care about the new Chanel bag or which shoes look better with which dress. I just want to get married and get on with life!'

I am sure the lament sounds familiar! Why is it that women lose the plot before getting married and treat money like a disease that they need to get rid of

ASAP? To be honest, I did spend a lot on my trousseau, making sure I had the perfect outfits, shoes and bags for every situation imaginable. There was just one minor problem—I didn't actually go through with the wedding! It's funny now, but you should have seen the look on my poor father's face, when he realized that he had just lost a minor fortune for nothing! It's interesting how many women face this problem today. They are so excited and caught up with the 'fun' and 'big-budget' element of the wedding that the more important stuff, such as 'who' they are marrying, is sidelined. In fact, just before I called off my wedding, my last thought was—*Oh shit, I should have bought the latest Berkin while I was at it!*

This transition from bride to bridezilla usually takes place a few months before the wedding. Our sweet lovable bride-to-be turns into Gabbar Singh, not willing to compromise on the Kareena-wala designer lehenga that costs more than a car or the diamond set that is worth a small flat in Mumbai, and is willing to kill for that honeymoon suite in that seven star hotel. Gone are the days, when brides were happy with the sariwallas from Chandni Chowk and a short honeymoon in Srinagar. Today, it is all about Tarun Tahiliani, Manav Gangwani and an upgrade at the Four Seasons! With a passion for fashion and a will to spill (the big bucks), we want it all! *Woh kehte hain na,* where there's a villa there's a way!

Unlike the past, nowadays, even grandmothers go wedding shopping, willing to experiment with new styles, wanting to look their best. We are not talking about the typical old saas-bahu serial addicts, or having-lost-the-will-to-live grandmas. These are the modern, stylish, pearl-string and chiffon-sari-wearing, bridge-playing, gym-going grandmoms, who know how to 'work it' even at the age of eighty plus. What a grandmother spends on herself now is what a bride used to spend on herself ten years ago. Clearly, expenditure on wedding wear tops the charts these days, due to a massive increase in disposable incomes, and an even more gigantic increase in human desires.

So, while the wedding planning team members are busy busting their ass to ensure the smooth execution of the bride and groom's every desire, the bride and groom themselves are busy dealing with their own demons. Let's start with bridezilla and her lifelong 'dream'—the trousseau! The wonderfully romantic-sounding collection of paraphernalia has made a comeback, and how!

Trousseau, originally a French term, defines the possessions a bride acquires before her wedding. It is a fancier version of packing for college. Remember your first semester at university? Your parents made sure you had everything that you would ever need. Lists were prepared to ensure that nothing was overlooked. Clothes, shoes, books, medicines, emergency cash, a debit card and last, but not the least, tonnes of food. Bottles of achaar, hundreds of parathas, thousands of packets of ready-to-eat food, such as dal makhani, keema pulao, navratan korma and chicken curry. Such highly detailed planning provided some solace for overprotective parents, who were highly anxious at the thought of their little ones finally flying away to another continent where they would have to look after themselves without the assistance of seven servants. In fact, most parents would take the fourteen-hour flight to go and drop off their kids, teach them how to make their beds, throw out the garbage and deal with the bank without Papa's help. Now, a decade later, the same parents are making detailed lists for wedding shopping. Indian parents... you gotta love them! Can't live with them, can't live without them!

This entire trousseau business started with parents determined to make sure their daughter had everything she needed for the wedding, honeymoon and the first few years of marriage. It was altogether common to see parents buying items like gold ornaments or decorative tea sets in instalments over the years, and keeping them aside for the start of a 'new chapter in her life'. I wonder how many brides wore a fancy tea set out to dinner, or invited people over just to display all the expensive bedspreads given by her parents! Practicality and usage aside, this collection of articles is what established initial perceptions about the bride, her upbringing and family status among her in-laws and other relatives. After all everyone should know *ki humaari bahu kitni ameer hai*! How forward thinking is that? We have always been so modern and wise. This is the reason India has the fewest number of divorces, but the highest number of boom-patty, boom-patty-boom.

Traditionally, a trousseau list consisted of what a bride would wear during the wedding, plenty of new saris that screamed 'newly married', jewellery pieces passed on from her great-grandmother, fancy linen and bedspreads that enticed the couple to have lots of babies, and many other requirements for the house. I do not understand the point of this. Why would you need so much stuff unless you're moving to an empty house? Does your mother-in-law not have a tea set? Are your in-laws short on cash? Can they not afford to get you a nice bedspread or proper linen? Are the local sari stores closing down after your wedding? I am not against this concept, but I must ask if a bride *really* needs 150 saris, twenty sets of jewellery, five fancy dinner sets, twelve 'toosh shawls, six sets of bedspreads, twelve towels, a new music system, a big television, a small car and a big house where all this can fit. But, as I say throughout this book, we are not big on logic and we love to blindly follow patterns that were made by a bunch of prehistoric creatures.

Over the past few decades, the term, 'trousseau' has

taken on a life of its own and brides these days spend shockingly obnoxious amounts of cash collecting all sorts of rubbish, out of which at least 50 per cent is never used or even looked at again. Nowadays, trousseau shopping starts at Emporio (the most expensive designer mall in New Delhi), continues in Dubai and ends in London. Designer lehengas cost much more than an entire wedding would cost thirty years ago. These days it's hard to find a nice wedding lehenga for less than ₹10,00,000. True story. My own wedding lehenga cost over ₹11,00,000 and is sitting in some warehouse outside New Delhi, waiting for the day it will be worn. Designers compete with each other to share a piece of this multi-crore pie. Bagging the order for the trousseau of a single high-profile wedding can rake in more moolah than the combined sale of a prêt line over the entire year. Diggity!

Wedding shopping covers the basics such as the wedding lehenga, sangeet outfit, mehndi outfit and appropriate clothing and jewellery for all the other gazillion pre-wedding parties. In addition, brides also like to check out what's new in the world of fashion. So, tickets are booked and bags are packed and before you know it, you're either at the MAC counter in the Dubai Mall or at the bridal section at Harrods. Needless to say, the purpose of these trips is to acquire as much stuff as possible without the bank cancelling your credit card and your father disinheriting you.

Since I do not want to be sued for defamation, I shall use my sister as a case study of 'a bride gone wild' while trousseau shopping. A couple of months before her wedding, she suddenly realized that she 'needed' the following—eighty-eight pairs of shoes, twenty-four evening clutches, fourteen Chanel bags, 138 different shades of eyeshadow, every single piece of lingerie available at Victoria's Secret, seven pairs of jeans, thirty-four new dresses, eighteen fancy gowns, four new overcoats (it's cold living all the way up on the seventeenth floor of a penthouse), fifteen new lipsticks from MAC, two new hair irons, three curling irons, twelve swimsuits, forty sarongs, 400 pairs of earrings—and fifty large suitcases to fit in all the shopping. Needless to say, we spent four days at the Dubai Mall, absolutely shocked by our capacity to spend our father's hard-earned money. Actually, my sister spent most of the money, with me as the glorified sidekick. I was allowed to spend 10 per cent of whatever she spent and thanks to her crazy bridezilla behaviour—I came back with a new wardrobe! I do enjoy the perks of being the bride's sister. It involves all the fun of being a bride, minus the responsibility and headache of it.

Unlike in the past, these days no one believes in making lists. You just go to the mall, and buy everything you like. Even if you don't need something, you buy it.

Why? Because you're getting married, dawg, and this is your last chance to milk your poor father dry!

While the bride is busy pumping new cash into the growing economy, the groom is looking for a large drink and a good shrink. But before I go into all that, let me first explain to you how men think and what they feel about shopping. You know the feeling when you wake up in the morning with a splitting headache, struggling to remember what happened the night before, after you had your twenty-seventh Café Patron shot? That's exactly how your guy feels when you tell him to go shopping with you. He tries hard to remember why he fell in love with you in the first place and how the eff love translates into death-by-Berkin. Men are simple creatures. They want food when hungry, sex when horny and a drink when thirsty. Shopping is done on a strictly 'need-to' basis and a man has absolutely no desire to spend precious hours at a mall, deciding whether you look better in green or pink. He would rather go play golf with the boys, or drown himself in the bubble bath you drew for him as pre-honeymoon practice.

Unlike women, men do not spend weeks deciding what they need to wear during the wedding. They usually have one designer they like and are comfortable relying on him for all their needs. You will never hear a man say, 'I have to go for my fifth trial for the bandh gala.' Oh, no, no, no. The tailor records the groom's measurements, and the clothes are made accordingly. Men are not finicky about their clothes being fitted or slightly loose. As long as they are comfortable in what they are wearing, that's all that matters. I do not know any guy who has been for more than one trial for a particular outfit. In fact, most of the men I know literally wait until the last minute to go wedding shopping, getting it out of the way just days before the drama begins. This is the reason a groom cannot comprehend his bridezilla's madness when she starts acting like a complete nut, making trips abroad in order to procure stuff that has nothing to do with love or marriage.

Exit: sanity; enter: the therapist.

Illustration © Ankit Parikh

Illustration © Fiza Khan

PARTY COMMITTEE

a. Sweety Uncle &
Rana Aunty,
5th Jan. Dholki Dinner
{100 people}

b. Inder Uncle &
Dolly Aunty,
10th Jan. Masquerade
{500 people}

b. Akhil Uncle &
Shobha Aunty,
15th Jan.
COCKTAIL NIGHT
{200 people}

b. Ajay Uncle &
Malini Aunty,
12th Jan. SUFI NIGHT
{300 people}

b. Varun Uncle &
Poonam Aunty,
18th Jan.
DJ Dance NIGHT
{400 people}

b. Jitish Uncle &
Preeti Aunty,
20th Jan.
Bollywood NIGHT
{150 people}

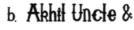

Illustration © Ankit Parikh

Illustration © Ankit Parikh

The MEHRAS and DUTTS

Invite you with great pleasure
to the wedding celebration of their children

Neelam   and   Keshav

DAUGHTER OF PREM   SON OF NEELA

& MEENA MEHRA   & DINESH DUTT

Natasha and Nikhil
Invite you to give blessings and joy to a
Wedding for

NEELAM and KESHAV

On: Thursday, the **26th of Feb 1982**

VALLAB HALL, AMBEDKAR ROAD, ANDHERI WEST, MUM

Sera Bandi - 3 pm
Assembly of Baraat - 3:30 pm
Pheras - 4 pm
Dinner: 7:30 pm

Illustration © Ankit Parikh

Illustration © Ankit Parikh

Illustration © Fiza Khan

The Bachelor's, the Bachelorette, the Youngsters': Party Time

$\mathcal{O}$nce upon a time, in a land not so far away, there was absolutely no concept of a youngsters' party, bachelor's or bachelorette. People did not even know what these words meant.

When my parents got married in 1981 (seems like a different era now), things functioned very differently. The pre-wedding excitement mostly consisted of—well nothing really! Most girls were not even allowed to get out of the house before the wedding, let alone traipse out of town for a bachelorette. The boys had a bit more freedom and some were allowed to indulge in just one night of 'all boys' fun. The friends threw a party for the groom, so that he could say goodbye to his single life, while ogling at mediocre-looking mujraawaalis. A couple of pegs of scotch, a few blue films and strange women dancing made the men feel really macho and hip. Where do you think the song *'Hume toh loot liya milke husn waalo ne'* came from? Oddly, this one night of limited freedom gave these frustrated men memories to last a lifetime, getting them ready to settle down with one woman. Or did it?

Fast forward to the present and we are happy with just about any excuse to get the hell out of town, or rather the country! A bachelor's party is not a one-night affair any more, at least not in the upper strata of society. Guys are not content with the traditional night out with the 'boys', painting the town pink. They want more, a lot more. So what do these men consider a legitimate bachelor's party? Well, I am certainly no expert, but from what I have seen amongst my own friends and acquaintances, I think I can safely say—at least one week of pure madness, where day and night merge into one. Even Hindi movies these days such as *Zindagi Na Milegi Dobara* are all about the fancy, once-in-a-life-time, epic bachelor trip! Remember Hrithik, Farhan and Abhay, driving around Spain in their fancy car and singing—*Oooh aaah, take the world and paint it red!*

So what is it that has brought about this maddening progression from mujraawaalis to strippers, from a few pegs of scotch to bottle service, from one semi-crazy night out in town to many epic nights in a foreign country, from seeing to touching, from Mumbai to Mykonos, and from hundred-rupee bills to unlimited cheap thrills? Is it because people have more money these days? Or are we missing significant information on this so-called legendary concept called the 'bachelor's'? What exactly are these men looking for?

Every year, several groups of men plan their ideal bachelor's vacation. These mostly happen in the European summer months, between July and September. Popular destinations for this kind of getaway include Ibiza, Mykonos, Vegas, Miami, Marbella, St Tropez, Krakow, Hvar and the new addition, Tomorrowland!

Tomorrowland, even though technically not the ideal bachelor destination, is the biggest and most popular music festival in the world, with over 4,00,000 people attending, thirteen stages and fifty artists. A one-hour drive from Brussels and you get to see all new age living legends, from David Guetta to Avicii to Afrojack, all performing as they have never done before. It has become a status symbol these days to attend this thunderous three-day festival. Tell a bunch of people that you have been to Tomorrowland and you will get the appreciation and validation you have been looking for all your life. Actually, I would like to rephrase that, as most people these days suffer from a hypo-'critical' condition called FOMO (Fear of Missing Out) and will secretly curse you for having experienced something that they still have not! Ouch!

Coming back to the boys, the average duration of a bachelor's vacation is about seven to ten days, covering two to three different cities or islands. Individual deluxe suites are booked in the best hotels available, as the guys would rather drown in the ocean than share their room with a friend. How else would they bring gorgeous, easily available women back to the room for some much-earned 'playtime'? *Woh kehte hain na*—you're not cheating unless you get caught! The kind of pressure at these holidays is immense! It doesn't matter if you are single or married, if you are at a bachelor's party you gotta get very naughty! (Just to clarify—I am not saying that all married men cheat on their wives, but yes, a lot of them do! My definition of cheating is not restricted to sex; rather, it is anything that a man would be scared to share with his wife. I mean, if you can't tell your wife, why do it, right? But then again, what do I know? I've never been for one of these bachelor's parties, and I am not a man!)

The amount of money spent at a bachelor's could easily support a poor family for years—education, housing, health, the works! We are looking at the finest restaurants, the best clubs and the hottest hostesses. These clubs usually have a minimum spend of 3,000–4,000 euro/pounds/dollars for a table; of course, one always ends up spending a LOT more than that. I mean ten men, thirty bottles of Dom Pérignon—you do the math.

🡿

Enough about the men. Let's see what the superior sex is up to and how they deal with pre-wedding jitters.

Previously, a groom-to-be had the license to be sleazy, but god forbid if the bride even suggested having a little bit of fun with her gal-pals, there would be repercussions (unless the girl was one of the lucky few with cool parents). Again, this was linked to the age-old belief that men were family providers and women were meant to bear children and take care of the home. After all, a woman didn't have her own identity and was merely the prized possession of a man. Remember the old Hindi films, where the wives were 'pati-vrata' damsels and the husband's every wish was their command? The man could do as he pleased, be it drinking, smoking or womanizing, and the woman had to deal with it, literally worship her spouse, no matter how obnoxious or insufferable he was! There was even a song: '*Jo bhi hai, jaisa bhi hai, mera pati mera devta hai!*' Jesus! Just imagine the horror!

Nowadays, things are different. We are blessed with

images of a feisty Sonakshi Sinha, giving it off to Chulbul Pandey; a sizzling hot Deepika Padukone, blatantly and unapologetically enjoying life; and my favourite, whacky Parineeti Chopra, blowing the head off any man who dares to mess with her. Thanks to the media's portrayal of the sexes, and a consequent shift in perception, women are finally coming out of their shells, ready to show the men that they mean business! In fact, for the first time in the history of Homo sapiens, women are excelling beyond their wildest dreams—not only earning more than men, but also drinking, driving (not necessarily in that order), fooling around and, most importantly, going for *bachelorette* vacations.

The term 'bachelorette' has recently been coined from the term 'bachelor's', and is nothing but the female version of the all-male party—the same drill, but with girls instead. Women, tired of the men having all the fun, decided to get even in the name of equality. Gone are the days when a bride-to-be would be under house arrest, learning how to cook puri-aloo, and perfecting the art of recycling wrapping paper. Now, she can outdo the men in every sphere of life, and have fun. So while the men are busy sowing their wild oats in the name of a 'bachelor's', the women are not far behind, not any more!

It all began with the traditional 'hen's night'—which, to be honest, is quite lame now. A hen's night started when girls were not allowed to get out of the house, and hence had to do whatever they wanted in the privacy of their own home, or the homes of one of their friends. The girls would get together, perhaps sneak in some alcohol, exchange gossip, paint their nails and talk about sex the same way a child talks about candy—forbidden but delicious.

Slowly, with modernization, this concept evolved and turned into a night out, with lots of liquor, short dresses and, if you were lucky, even a male stripper! Then came globalization and it got much easier to get visas for foreign countries. To sum it up, visa + willingness to get the hell out of your comfort zone = start packing those bags because this is the age of bachelorette vacations!

I had a bachelorette a few years ago in Dubai, something I now regret. I mean—*Dubai?* Seriously? What a fool I was! But it taught me one thing and that is NEVER to have a bachelorette in a place where any kind of PDA is forbidden and everything shuts at 3 a.m. Restrictions aside, my eight gal pals and I had an unforgettable time! Good food, great wine, a remarkable nightlife and the best shopping ever—all the ingredients to satisfy a girl about to get married (the fact that I did not get married is the icing on the cake)! Sadly, there were no male strippers (it was the Middle East!) or whipped cream, but I didn't mind, as I am not really into that kind of stuff.

My sister, on the other hand, had the privilege of not one, but two bachelorettes (she *did* get married, phew)! One in Sardinia and one in Vegas! Talk about discrimination. I mean, same father, same bank account, but I was sent to shawarma-land, while she was busy getting her eyes examined due to too much eye-candy exposure (rich people's problems). I have been given strict instructions to keep quiet—so I cannot reveal what exactly happened—but it was Vegas and I do not need to say more. I will say one thing though, and that is, when my sister returned from her bachelorette part two, I believe her exact words were, 'Now I've seen it all!' Well, if you have seen it all at the age of twenty-five, good luck to your husband!

Another new trend is starting to pick up now, as we girls clearly have way too many friends—one bachelorette trip is just not enough, because friends are divided into categories. There are school friends, college friends, post-college/miscellaneous friends, work colleagues. No one wants to mix up groups, so instead, multiple plans are made and a huge contribution is made to the tourism industry. These poor little Daddy's girls, what a hard life, so many holidays and such little time! I used to be one of these girls. I miss those days.

So, coming to the point, what exactly happens during these 'girls just wanna have fun' vacations? Unlike a bachelor's (which is standard), a bachelorette has many facets. Every character has a different role and we need each one of them to complete this mad scenario. I have made a list.

The Crazy One Who Never Gets Tired

There is always at least one girl in the group, who can party like a rockstar on crack. She is normally the one who gets the party started, but is reluctant to trudge back to the hotel at the end of the night. She can drink and drink and drink, and then drink some more. Not all the alcohol distilleries in the world would be enough to get this one tired! She might be slightly difficult to manage, but is definitely needed to get things going!

The Funny One Who Does Get Tired

The funny one is essential, as—well, she is the one who is the most fun! As the crazy one retires during the day (she has to recharge for the night), the funny one takes over. She is the person making everyone laugh and helping them deal with the bitch of a hangover. This girl is great company even without alcohol and makes sure that everyone is cheerful no matter what.

The Sensible One Who Keeps Everyone in Check

There is always one girl in the group, who has her head on her shoulders and her brains intact. She is looking out for her friends, trying to ensure no one gets into trouble. She might not be the most popular one, but is definitely the glue holding the girls together. She does a head-count before leaving, so that nobody is left behind. She holds back your hair, while you vomit (the others are too drunk themselves). And she orders your hangover breakfast in the morning and gives you a sickness medicine. This is your mom in disguise.

The Shopaholic Who Shops Till She Drops

The shopaholic's main aim during a vacation is to shop! Be it during a bachelorette or a honeymoon, this one cannot start her day without first paying a visit to the nearest mall. She will wake up before everyone (even if it kills her) and get those new Jimmy Choo boots, before meeting the girls for lunch. She follows all the labels on Twitter and Instagram. You will never see this one repeat an outfit or a 'look'. She is proud to be ten steps ahead of her friends when it comes to fashion.

The Gym Addict Who is Loath to Miss Exercise

Familiar? We all have that one person (or more) in our lives who is totally obsessed with her body and would rather miss a heartbeat than a sweaty gym session. She is a complete gym junkie and cannot start her day without first sweating off a gallon. She is obviously super-fit and takes great pride in her ultra-toned body and glowing face. She will most certainly sneak back to the hotel, while the others are still getting shit-faced, so that she can wake up early the next morning and go for a run.

The Boring One Who Is a Complete Buzzkill

This one is tricky. There is always that one friend, who we have known for as long as we can remember. She is super-boring, but cannot be left out of the bachelorette. Mostly, friends just try to avoid her and are nice to her only when the guilt of being a horrible person starts kicking in. She doesn't talk much, and when she does, she is made to realize that she is better company with her mouth shut. She takes a selfie a minute and pretends to be having a great time!

The Complainer for Whom Nothing Is Good Enough

This girl who is never happy, because she has a constant FOMO. Not a single second goes by without this one moaning about something—'Are you sure this is the best hotel available?' 'Are you sure we can't get an upgrade?' 'This bathroom is so small!' 'This fish has bones!' 'This club sucks!' 'I absolutely refuse to travel business class! Chee!' The list is endless. After a while, all you want is the sweet release of death.

No matter how much fun or how irritating these girls are, no bachelorette is complete without these Seven Wonders of the World.

✒

Since I have already taken the plunge and risked losing most of my friends with these revelations, I might as well go all the way and acquaint you with what we call a youngsters'.

This was an idea that started when I was about ten years old. My mother's cousin, who lived in New York, was getting married in New Delhi, and decided to have a youngsters' party. I remember, at the time, it was a very new concept and the older generation had a hard time accepting that they would be automatically excluded from part of a wedding celebration, if over forty. They complained loudly, expressing their dismay at not being invited. The youngsters at the time did not care and still went ahead and organized the event. And that was that— the birth of a new trend that segregated the young ones from the elderly! It was not long before people started appreciating the carefree nature and craziness of the situation, and the trend spread like a wild forest fire.

As the years went by, with more and more parties just for youngsters, this concept too developed (like the bachelorette) and evolved into something unrecognizable and larger than life. Until five years ago, a youngsters' was still a party, but a rather lavish one. Hundreds of invited guests, many lakhs spent on décor, food, alcohol and a DJ—it became a legitimate wedding function. And as soon as it did, like most legitimate things in life, it lost its charm.

The youngsters these days like a challenge, and anything that's too easy to attain is not worth having. Therefore, even the youngsters' party must grow in complexity. Once again, we are in the visa line, booking our tickets and getting ready to party in Spain, Italy, Turkey or wherever it is that our hosts' imagination and bank balance takes us. The only difference is that this time there will be at least a hundred people (unlike a small bachelor's/bachelorette group) being hosted and treated to the best of the best that life has to offer.

Apart from the plane tickets, *everything* is taken care of. It's almost akin to being a celebrity. Imagine landing in Ibiza with a fancy pick up waiting for you, and reaching a five star hotel in a luxury car. The standard duration of a youngsters' is three days/nights, and professionals plan every minute of this opulent stay. From lunch, to dinner, to bars, to clubs, to chilling by the pool—every single aspect of this legendary three-day vacation is presented to the guests on a golden platter.

In 1905, Albert Einstein taught us that $E=MC^2$, which meant, Energy = Mass x the speed of light squared. This is common knowledge that everybody has access to. What people do not have access to is a new formula, created by the crème de le crème of our rapidly growing society; according to this formula, $E=M+C^2$. In other words, Excitement = Money + Chutiya-panti (squared). This means that lots of money is required to create any form of excitement nowadays, which brings us to the next element of our formula, the chutiya, who is willing to spend all that cash. The bigger the chutiya = more money = more excitement, so in short, $E=M+C^2$! I knew all the science

I learnt in school wouldn't go in vain!

Needless to say, I myself have been the chutiya of this equation a number times. And I hope I will be able to return to my fabulous hosts all the great times that I have been blessed with, thanks to them. When I wonder what I have done to deserve all the free holidays abroad every now and then, I realize—I have made the right friends! So the bottom line: chutiya is awesome!

At some level, I applaud this magnificent transition caused due to rising levels of income and exposure. The tourism industry is thriving as never before and rich Indians have a huge role to play. We have not even reached the wedding and there have already been five trips abroad—the proposal, trousseau shopping, the bachelor's, bachelorette and youngsters'!

Yet, there's a flip-side. The word 'celebration' has many new meanings attached to it, some of which do not feature in the dictionary. While a celebration these days signifies huge amounts of money being spent, on the other hand, it indicates that people are getting more and more disconnected from each other. Why is it that we need to keep running away from reality? Is it really that bad? Or are we just running away from ourselves? Why is it that the words 'epic' and 'legendary' are only associated with parties in Spain or Greece? And why is it that whatever happens locally is immediately labelled as 'lame' and 'boring'?

The answer is very simple—we do this because we can. Our fathers and grandfathers were much too busy to plan holidays, since they were toiling, trying to ensure that *we* secured a fabulous life. While we are a lucky lot—for, our ancestors looked out for us—the impact has been detrimental. We are so handicapped by our privileges that we cannot even begin to appreciate the small things in life. We are so blinded by material comfort that we just do not know how to look beyond it. That purpose in life, that drive, that ambition, that fire in the belly that we hear our fathers talk about is completely missing from our lives. After all, many people from my generation have never had to work for anything! Everything has been given to us on a diamond platter and unfortunately, we don't value it.

I am not against taking vacations abroad (whatever the excuse might be); in fact, I thoroughly enjoy it. I would rather travel business class than donate the money to charity. And it's much more enjoyable to 'find' yourself in a limo, sipping vintage Dom Pérignon, rather than slumming it out in some ashram in Dharamshala.

But I have to say—I am perplexed by the approach that values surnames more than personality, a bank balance more than credibility, and clothes more than character. Let's enjoy our blessings, but not forget who we are, where we come from and where we are going.

And with that let's involve ourselves with the most controversial, most fun and most competitive part of a wedding—the dance practice!

Dance Practice:
The Self-obsession Test

It's one month before the wedding; the bride and groom are getting some serious panic attacks. One would think these are pre-wedding jitters, but that's not it. The 'broom' (bride and groom) is stressing over the sangeet night performance!

It's ironic how these days pre-wedding jitters take place after the honeymoon, because until then, everyone is too busy! Once the wedding planning, shopping, bachelor's, bachelorette and youngsters' are all done with, it's time for the real competition! Brace yourselves because the much awaited dance practice begins! I am sure most of you know what I am talking about, but for those who do not, let me explain. The sangeet function is meant to be the crazy one, with lots of entertainment. Traditionally, a few family members would get together and prepare a few dance numbers and songs that would be performed to entertain the guests. Everything about this performance was extremely casual, with the best dancer/singer in the family training the others. It was a short and sweet performance, mostly teasing the bride and groom, and the guests were thoroughly entertained (the standards were pretty low back then). There was no organized dance practice as such, as families stayed together during weddings and everyone had access to each other 24x7.

These days, dance practice sessions are serious business. Unlike the good ol' days when family members got involved, now everything is done professionally and nothing is possible without the best choreographer. Professional choreographers are not cheap and charge anything between ₹1,500 and ₹3,000 an hour! That's definitely a lot of money for a wedding performance. I mean, it's not a red carpet situation, is it? Despite this, we refuse to lower the bar. When my sister got married, we spent over ₹80,000 on the choreographer, and I know people who have spent lakhs flying down the best ones from Bollywood.

Organizing a dance practice is not for the faint-hearted. It's a daily battle, where—unlike in a casino—

the house always loses! Fortunately (ha!), I have been a part of hardcore dance practice sessions for over ten different weddings, out of which I was made 'in charge of entertainment' for seven. Short of pulling my hair out, I did everything else I could to keep my nerves calm.

The first challenge is to make a list that includes everyone—friends, family, family friends, parents' close friends, sisters'/brothers' close friends…and the list goes on. The next challenge is to *actually* get everyone together, and this is a royal pain in the backside. Some people are free in the mornings; the others are only free in the evenings. For some, Sunday works, and for others, any day but Sunday! It's a logistical nightmare and the host goes bonkers trying to coordinate the schedules of fifty different people.

Once we are able to accomplish this daunting task, there is the next challenge slyly waiting—and that is to actually get everyone to dance. This is no joke either, as people have very strong preferences about:

1. Whom they want to dance with. This is a big problem, as everyone does not necessarily get along with each other. When assigning people to different songs, it's better to put friends together in a group, or else you are inviting a whole lot of unnecessary politics. In other words, you're screwed!

2. What songs they want to dance to. Once again, some people like fast songs; some prefer slower numbers. And if you don't cater to these whims then say goodbye to your sanity.

3. Where they are placed in the dance. I was once in charge of a friend's dance practice and I felt like the warden of a mental asylum. I witnessed some surreal fights springing from the most hilarious of situations—a girl wanted to be placed 'centre front' instead of 'left back'. (I still have no idea what that means.) Then another wanted her right side profile to be more prominent than the left; yet another one, let's call her 'A', objected to the dance position of 'B', as she considered herself closer to the bride and wanted to be standing up front (psycho alert!).

After having the privilege of witnessing such drama, I must wonder if, in fact, we have grown up. In school, we fought over basketball teams and now, we fight for our rightful place on the dance floor and in our friends' hearts.

After successfully managing the people on the dance floor, we move on to yet another challenge, and that is making sure that the choreographer is on the same page. We don't want a shabby performance, but at the same time, one has to realize that this is *not* the Filmfare

Awards. These are regular people dancing at a wedding function, and the steps should be taught accordingly.

Last year, I had to learn some fancy steps for a very close friend's wedding and it drove me up the wall. I am not the best dancer (not even close) and it was a complete nightmare. To make matters worse, I had a panic attack on the day, as something had not occurred to me earlier— the fact that I would be dancing in a goddamn sari! All the steps that I had mastered in my 'Juicy's' suddenly did not seem that simple, turning me into a complete nervous wreck. No doubt, I messed up at the performance, as I was more concerned with keeping my sari on, as opposed to getting the dance steps right. Now, I have stopped dancing, choosing alternate methods of making a fool of myself in front of a thousand people.

↙

Now, if you think getting fifty people to coordinate itineraries and cooperate is tough, and getting a choreographer to do his job is even harder, try writing a script that weaves together all the performances, and talks about the bride and groom without getting too emotional—ensuring that the guests laugh more than they cry.

The sangeet night performance, until quite recently,

consisted of a bunch of people dancing to some fun numbers: a romantic number to which the bride and groom would usually dance (*'Ishq Wala Love'* type); a slow song to which either the bride herself or one of her closest friends would perform (*'Afreen'* or *'Jashn-e-bahara'*, or of a similar genre); and three to four fast-paced, fun songs to which the remaining friends and family would dance. Sometimes, a family member would give a short speech or toast that was very touching and would guarantee waterworks, not just from the couple in question, but also the guests. Somehow, I didn't quite understand or enjoy this method of entertainment. If I wanted to cry I would go and watch one of Karan Johar's films, not attend a sangeet!

I knew that if I were in charge, copious tears would be done away with! And so began the era of laughter. My foray into such emceeing started in 2009—when I accidentally wrote a script for a close friend's sangeet performance. My writing was funny, with just the right amount of humour and sufficient importance given to the couple—so as to make them feel special minus the waterworks.

As this school of thought gained popularity, all my friends wanted me to come on stage and make fun of them (with love, of course), revealing their funny stories, with the rest of the friend-performers coming and dancing after every new revelation. Suddenly, I was the emcee for every wedding, going mental writing scripts for two to three couples at one time, even those I barely knew! It was 'KILLERRR' as the Delhiites would say and the new trend blossomed, making dance practice more chaotic than ever. In fact, it gave birth to a new kind of competition in my world of weddings—the girls' side versus the boys' side. In other words, who could entertain better?

On one occasion, a handful of grooms wanted me to emcee from their side, saying, 'Dude, the girl's side is practising really hard, we need you to kick their ass!' While I was still processing this information, I got a call from the bride-to-be, who was in panic mode, screaming, 'Babeeeee, you have to write my script, I've heard the boys are doing some amazing stuff, we have to be better than them!' God have mercy on the poor writer! While this was all very flattering for me, it also caused severe anxiety and it became my life's mission not to disappoint the soon-to-be married couple.

Then there was my sister's wedding! One month before her big day, I played host to approximately twenty thousand dance practice sessions, and almost forgot what normal life felt like. Every evening at 7 p.m., I would take my laptop and go down to the garden so that I could write my sisters' sangeet performance script and supervise the domestic help as they set up the place to get it ready for practice. It was very entertaining to watch everyone, from the sweeper to the cook, eagerly connecting the music system, doing sound checks, making sure the microphone worked and creating enough space in the garden for all the dancers to fit comfortably. The onlookers were very excited to be part of this circus, and watched us as we struggled to learn Bollywood steps, such that we would make Yo Yo Honey Singh proud. (Incidentally, these days, nine out of ten hit songs are by the man himself; he seems to have cracked some kind of shaadi code, because his songs are the most played at every single Indian wedding!)

Let me give you a snapshot of what I went through before my sister's wedding: eleven drafts of the script, making sure no one was forgotten and equal importance was given to both families; coordinating and getting eight different groups of people to learn the steps of fourteen different songs; making sure everyone knew the order of the songs on performance night; and sitting for hours and hours with the sound and light person, sorting out audio as well as other special effects such as the confetti and fireworks—after all, each beat and every dance move needs to be synchronized with the appropriate effect. It is no less than a concert! Gone are the days of 'simple' Hindustan, we are now living in the Times of (Rich) India.

Once the dance practice begins, everything is utterly chaotic. Yet, all the participants are on the ball—learning steps, coordinating movements with the other dancers, and making sure that they are eating right, so that they look *hot* while performing. Wedding fever literally takes over and no amount of Crocin or Combiflam helps, until the wedding is over and the couple has left for their honeymoon.

Performance mania is not restricted to the youngsters, with quite a few aunties and uncles secretly excited about performing on stage. I realized this during my sisters' dance practice sessions and was very amused. Every time I'd ask my parents' friends to perform one of the dance numbers, they'd look very shy and say, 'No, no, how can I do this?' But deep down, I knew I could lure them into the rabbit hole—and lure them, I did. After these once-shy aunties and uncles would agree to dance, they'd become a force to be reckoned with. Until they hit perfection with every move and expression, they'd keep practising and drive the poor choreographer up the wall.

During these practice sessions, the aunties stop eating carbohydrates for fear of looking fat on stage. A strict protein diet and cellulite reduction treatment before the wedding, and the aunties are all set to shine in their backless cholis; considerably escalating the temperature until *aadmiyon ke paseeney choot jaye* even in the freezing months of December–January. (As a side note, it's incredible how women these days take so much care of themselves, looking not a day over thirty-five, no matter what their chronological age may be. Most of my mother's friends are so well maintained they look younger and dress better than my friends and me. A low carb diet for a flat stomach, regular gym work-outs for a toned body and a closet full of Roberto Cavalli, Oscar de la Renta and Tarun Tahiliani—you're all set no matter what age!)

The uncles, on the other hand, not so concerned about their curls and curves, are constantly trying to outdrink the youngsters and re-live their own youthful obnoxious days. Their size-zero wives take a back seat, while they happily reminisce about the days gone by when 'sex on the beach' was not a cocktail and weekends in Europe were not the norm. On one dance practice evening, I remember my father innocently comparing the story of the film, *Dil Chahta Hai*, to his younger years, when two of his overweight best friends and he drove around the Western Ghats in their old Fiat. Of course, my sister and I choked at this comparison, not sure what we were more horrified about—the fact that Dad was once young or the fact that he thought this story was worth sharing!

The truth is that during wedding season, people forget their age, indulging in all sorts of fun activities. Different age groups merge, judgements are temporarily suspended, and blinkers are worn so that one can see only what one wants to. It's brilliant.

🖎

Every dance practice is like a party with lots of food, dancing and a fully stocked bar. Alcohol is essential as it acts like the glue that holds everyone together, making them get along—even with those whom they find most intolerable. A bar also helps one cope with the stress of dancing, kill all inhibitions and set the body free!

Along with a well-stocked bar, the host is compelled to present an elaborate food menu. Long hours of jumping and twisting build up an appetite and the guests look forward to a delicious selection of snacks. These 'snacks' can range from kathi rolls, burgers and pizzas to more elaborate menus with biryani, nihari, dal makhani, butter chicken and so on. Healthy options such as quinoa and breadless sandwiches are mandatory now, as women run away from carbs faster than Milkha Singh and P.T. Usha put together.

Once again, I have risked the wrath of my friends and revealed to you what a typical big-budget wedding entails—a series of lavishly hosted dance practice sessions that start early in the evening and end early in the morning! To be honest, it is a lot of fun (unless you are the unfortunate host) and does a great job of setting the mood for the upcoming nuptials.

I have prepared a small test, which will tell you if you are self-obsessed and to what degree. Sure, we are all a little self-absorbed, but when we cross that imaginary line and go over to 'bonkersville', there is cause for concern.

The Self-obsession Test

1. When in conversation with someone, how many times do you start a sentence with 'I'?
   a) Never—I prefer listening to others.
   b) Sometimes.
   c) Always—if I am not the centre of the conversation, I am not in the conversation!

2. On an average, how many times do you change your outfit before going to a party?
   a) Zero. Who does that?
   b) Not more than once, unless I look like what the cat dragged in!
   c) As many times as required, until I am perfectly satisfied.

3. How many times a week do you visit the beauty/men's salon?
   a) I don't need to go to a salon!

b) Once a week/fortnightly—I need to look good for the weekend!

c) I live at the beauty salon—you think I was born flawless?

4. You have to attend a function and realize you have a pimple developing on your forehead. What do you do?

a) It's a pimple not a bomb—I put on some make-up and get on with things.

b) I go to my dermatologist and take his/her advice.

c) Panic attack—all social niceties are suspended until further notice.

5. After a holiday, you realize you have put on five kilos. What do you do?

a) It's normal to gain weight during a holiday; I will get back to normal in time.

b) Oh no, my jeans are tight! I hit the gym and stock up on fruits and vegetables.

c) I go on a strict juice diet and don't put any solid food in my mouth, until I am back to size zero.

Congratulations, once again for looking within and proudly embracing your virtues along with your vices. One without the other can lead to perfection and that, my dear readers, can get very boring.

Mostly a's — Hello darling! Are you even alive?

If your answers are mostly a's, then you need 'design' intervention ASAP! According to my test, you don't like talking about yourself at all; you don't care what you look like when going out and you never visit the salon. While I am a huge fan of Mother Nature, I think there's no harm in getting a manicure or a blow-dry once in a while. I am aware of the concept of inner beauty, but a little grooming every now and then won't hurt anyone! Remember, while you do not have to look at yourself, others do!

Mostly b's — The perfect mix of inner and outer beauty. BINGO!

If your answers are mostly b's, you are confident and secure in your own skin. You have your own opinion on matters and are not scared to voice them, and are also smart enough to know when to shut up. You like to look good and groom yourself accordingly, but are not obsessed with your appearance. You will go that extra mile once in a while, but your life is not dependent on the latest Dior bag or the new liposuction technique. The beauty parlour is a place you visit on weekends, but is not your second home!

Mostly c's — Who said Michael Jackson is dead?

If your answers are mostly c's, then I don't mean to be harsh but, oh dear! First, you need a BIG hug. Second, you need to love yourself for the way you are. Looking perfect on the outside is just a temporary solution to not feeling perfect on the inside. You lose interest in a conversation if it doesn't involve you; a pimple is enough to bring life to a halt; and your second home is the beauty salon. Something is not right and self-obsession is never the solution. Figure out why you have this incessant need to always look ten years younger and why you are not able to embrace yourself the way you are.

🖋

We are done with the wedding planning, trousseau shopping, international celebrations, and last but not the least—dance practice! We are now ready to attend the wedding, but it's not that simple. As you have seen, we do everything in style and every wedding function has a pre-party and is followed by an after party! So what the hell are we waiting for? Let's get started!

THE INDIAN WEDDING MENU

Appetizer - Non Veg

Golden Fried Prawns
Fried salt Calamari
Rawai Fry fish fingers
Murgh Malai Tikka
Gilawati Kebab
Gosht Shammi Kebab
Ajwaini fish Tikka
Hara Kolmi (Prawns)
Gosht seekh Kebab
Chicken Tikka Afghani

Appetizer - Veg

Paneer Tikka Masala
Hara Bhara Kebab
Gobhi ki Tehari
Hing Wale Aloo
Cheese Corn Ball
Fish cake with a Thai Chilli dip
Spring Rolls- veg
Coconut Shrimp
Corn Fritters

Main Course - Non Veg

Laal Maas
Awadhi Fish Qorma
Nahari Gosht
Chhooza Makhani
Mahi Tikka Tandoori
Masaledar Chaamp

Chicken Curry
Methi Murg
Crab Curry
Beef Stew
Achari Murg
Malabar Chicken Curry

Illustration © Ankit Parikh

Kacche Gosht Ki Biryani

Lagan Ka Murgh

Goan Prawn Curry

Chicken Cafreal

Prawn Balchao

Mutton Vindaloo

Chicken Xacutti

Balchao Naan

Raan e Khyberi

Chicken Biryani

Chicken Dahiwala

Chicken croquette

GRILLS

Red Snapper with
Jalapeno chilli

Grilled Sea Bass

Lamb chops

Pasta and Risotto Section

2 Handmade Pasta (Fettuccini/ Ravioli)

3 proprietary pasta (Penne/ Fuisili/ Spaghetti) with Chicken/Prawns/
Fish and Pomodoro basilico / Pesto /Aglio olio /Cheese sauce

Accompaniments

Porcini mushroom/ Truffle oil / Smoked salmon

Salad Bar

Smoked salmon platter

Chicken Salad with Pesto Sauce

Assorted salad greens and crisp seasonal vegetables
dressings and condiments, Salad caprese,Tandoori
aloo chana chat,carrot Koshimbir, boondi raita
papad, achaar, chutney

Scottish smoked salmon platter

Washington apple salad with greens

Sprouted Bean Salad

MAIN COURSE - NON VEG

Channa Masala
Dhingri Mutter
Shahi Subz Biryani
Aloo Katliyan
Bhindi Nayantara
Makai Shezaadi
Achari Paneer
Aloo Poshto
Baby Corn and Paneer Jalfrazie
Baby Corn Palak
Baingan Methi ki Subzi
Baked Paneer in Tomato Sauce
Bhindi Sambhariya
Bhindi Masala
Cabbage and Capsicum Subzi
Carrot Methi Subzi

Pizza with different
toppings on circulation
Bouquetiere of veggies
Melanzane with kheema
Aloo Mirchi Ka Salan
Vegetarian Xacutti
Vegetable Caldin
Khatti Dal

Vegetable Biryani
Vegetable Croquette
Dhingri Mutter
Miloni Tarkari
Dal Makhni

Mexican fried rice with
refried beans and jalapeno
Assorted Indian and
Mexican Breads

Illustration © Ankit Parikh

CHAT COUNTER

Pani Poori
Bhel Poori
Sev Poori
Ragda Patties
Aloo Papdi
Goan Vegetable Paella
Aloo Anardana Pocket roll station
Cutting Chai
Dahi Batata Puri
Aloo Puri
Uttapa

Keema Kulcha
Goan Seafood Paella
Chola Bhature
Pau Bhaji
Vada Pau
Dosa (masala/ kheema)
Ice gola station
Juice float bar
Tender coconut (on site)
Grilled Veg Sandwitch
Tikka Rolls
Dhokla

DESSERTS COUNTER

Mexican Brownie

Blueberry & strawberry Mousse

Sticky toffee pudding [with custard]

Assorted Ice Cream (3 flavors)

Jalebi

Kulfi Bar in Kullhad

Phirnee

Assorted Cheese cakes

Tiramisu

Bebinca

Assorted Ice Creams

Gulab Jamun

Rasmalai

Gulab Patti Sandesh by Guest

Kesariya Doodh

AND THE LIST CONTINUES

Illustration © Ankit Parikh

Illustration © Fiza Khan

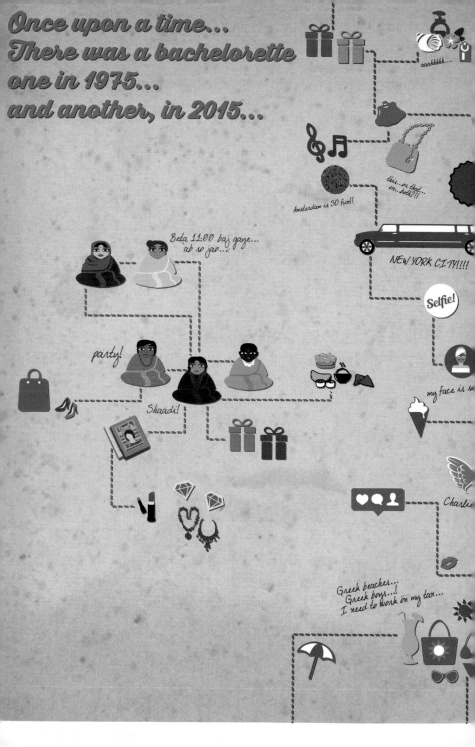

Illustration © Fiza Khan

Illustration © Fiza Khan

Pre - wedding Ceremonies:
The Official Madness Begins

The countdown has begun. It's ten days until the wedding and things are about to get mental. Actually, 'mental' is an understatement, as these days, people need to get their livers insured before a big wedding.

Now, all events, pre-wedding or otherwise, begin and end with alcohol. The amount of alcohol consumed at each function (big or small) would be considered humanly impossible a decade ago—considering there was no Honey Singh, promoting vodka and champagne and encouraging people to party all night! Instead, we had Pawan Singh singing songs like '*Puja puja, bhog chadao, bhog chadao*'; an attitude that encouraged people to visit the temple; and a strong emphasis on human values, highlighting the role of the lord almighty in every life situation, especially marriage.

Interestingly, nowadays, everything is anti-sanskaar. Even Bollywood songs highlight the importance of being 'cool', with lyrics such as '*Dope karo, sex karo, daaru piyo, gaadi chalao!*' Even a dharmic number such as '*Tum hi ho bandhu*' has been remade into a wild party song in the movie *Cocktail*, with hundreds of intoxicated people jumping up and down in their sexy swimwear, trying to get laid. We are witnessing a time where Viagra has replaced values, guns have replaced god, and people choose to have a large peg of Grey Goose rather than a sip of Ganga-jal.

The amount of liquor consumed at one wedding party is probably what was consumed throughout the entire wedding season in the past. Alcohol has slowly but surely made its way to the top of the list, as far as celebration priorities are concerned, and everyone (men, women, boys and girls) is completely annihilated throughout a wedding. In the 1980s and 1990s, the parents of the bride and groom were concerned with which flowers had been ordered and which ladoos tasted better. Now, no one gives a rat's ass about arbitrary stuff like that. Parents are far more concerned about ensuring a fully stocked bar that will never be depleted no matter what—the first rule of any successful party. We Delhiites have a profound saying:

Hum khattam ho jayengey, parr yeh bar nahi khattam hoga!

The only issue is this—the older we get the harder it is to drink night after night and wake up in the morning and work. So, the way we deal with this problem is that we just stop working! We will quit our jobs, but will never miss a single wedding function. The logic being: 'We will get another job, yaar, but this wedding will not happen again.' Big time FOMO!

Luckily, many people from the upper strata of society don't have to work and therefore, this problem doesn't exist (phew). Just to clarify: it's not like we don't want to work—we do—but we just don't have the time for work. I mean, think about it, from October to March, we are busy attending weddings; then from April to June, we are busy recovering from these weddings; and then from July to September, we are 'killing it' in Europe—'Arre bhai, summer holiday hai and India is like so yuckyyy!' So where is the time to work? This is also a good time to clear the misconception about Indians being lazy. You attend one Indian wedding and you will see how much effort it requires; a lazy person wouldn't last a day!

I recently attended a close friend's wedding, and thirty of his college friends flew down to New Delhi, all the way from the States, to attend this multi-day extravaganza. They were very excited to see what an actual Indian wedding was like, especially when they were sent the itinerary, which had a minute-by-minute schedule for the next seven days. They were absolutely blown away by our Indian hospitality and our capacity to party. They were also very intrigued by our clothes, jewellery and the fact that all the women looked as if they have just walked out of a bridal couture/liposuction catalogue. One of the American friends, who was very amused by this scenario said, 'It really is an art—to look like a goddess, yet behave like a dangerous animal!' Each guest went back to the States with some body part not functioning. Some had wedding injuries, some were bitten by dogs (warning: don't try to pet a dog when inebriated), and the rest needed a liver transplant. Most of them were so tired by the time the actual wedding day dawned that we had to give them injections of Café Patron to keep them awake and alive! You really have to be an Indian to understand:

a) the concept of logic
b) the logic behind so many pre-wedding events

So…what does this pre-wedding rollercoaster look like and what goes down in these ten days, before the actual wedding? In this chapter, I am taking you into the world of pre-wedding action, day-by-day and step-by-step.

Traditionally, pre-wedding gatherings or 'open houses' were organized to entertain the out of town guests, who would come down especially for the wedding. These daily open houses created an enjoyable environment and distracted the parents of the bride who, even while being secretly relieved, had to portray a sense of sadness at the thought of giving away their daughter.

The bride's and groom's respective homes turned into the 'shaadi ka ghar', with constant activity and excitement for at least a week before the actual wedding day. The women of the house played the dholki and sang songs teasing the bride and groom, especially making fun of the bride's future mother-in-law. Bearing in mind the relationship between a mother-in-law and daughter-in-law is similar to the relationship between India and Pakistan, this was clearly not the best way to start the delicate equation. But as a wise sardarji once said, '*Kuch nahi hota, yaar.*' It was probably the only time one could get away with murder!

We Indians love to sing, and have a song for every situation imaginable. Back in the day, there were songs advising the bride about how best to please her husband and mother-in-law; how to convert her groom into a henpecked husband from a momma's boy; and how to manipulate the mom-in-law into doing all the housework. There'd be counter-attack songs telling the mother-in-law how to keep her new daughter-in-law in check and remain in the position of power—*kyunki saas bhi kabhi bahu thi!* (An Indian mother may make a million sacrifices for her son, but will die before she lets another woman take her place.) We are also the proud lyricists of many songs making fun of the groom and his inability to please both his mom and wife (*din mein respect karengey, raat mein sex karengey*), and finally, songs that warn the bride-to-be about the perils of marriage—the biggest one being boredom.

While the women of the house were busy singing and dancing, the men would enjoy their Patiala pegs, feel bad for the groom, and secretly check out the beautiful wives of other men. After all, we have a saying: *Khud ke bacche aur doosre ki biwi bahut ache lagte hain!* (Men love their own kids and other men's' wives, the most).

Open houses, back in the day, started early, around 7 p.m., and the night ended by 11 p.m. Midnight was considered a *very* late night, and every day was a Sunday, until the wedding.

Coming back to the present, one cannot imagine a wedding without at least a month of celebrations, prior to the D-day. Open houses are still a very important part of the pre-wedding action. But like everything else, this too, has evolved beyond recognition.

Nowadays, an open house is just another name for

debauchery with at least a hundred people, a lavish spread prepared by the best caterer in town and enough alcohol to fill up the Arabian Sea. Kicking off around midnight, these parties can go on until the wee hours of the morning, thanks to songs like, *'Chaar baj gaye, lekin party abhi baaki hai!'* I bow down to Sir Honey Singh. Seriously, what would we do without his gyaan?

The women of the house singing and playing the dholki have now been replaced by professional dholki guys, who come dressed up, looking like shiny disco balls, in groups of four to six. These men really know how to get a party started. They beat our dholkis with much vigour and passion, sing one Punjabi wedding song after the other, make up their own versions of the latest Bollywood numbers and take us back to the golden-olden era.

I have actually heard these dholki guys go nuts on advertisement jingles for brands like Nirma and Lijjat Papad. You do not want to miss watching guests do the moves on *'Nirma, Nirma, washing powder nirma, dhoodh si safedi nirma se aayi, sab ki pasand Nirma!'* Just shows us that we, as north Indians, are insane and will dance to pretty much anything, as long as it doesn't make sense. Well, sense or no sense, the dholki guys get the job done, as nowadays, people respond better to beats than to words. In addition, these guys are given a list of names that they need to call out, and one by one all the close family members and friends are made to stand up and dance rigorously to the beats of this legendary instrument. It's a great way to get everyone excited and pumped up for the wedding.

↙

Besides dholki nights, close friends and family throw for the couple a steady flow of theme parties like 'the black tie event', a 'masquerade ball', 'going retro' and so on. This is when all the Oscar de la Renta gowns come out of the closet and the Harry Winston jewels leave the locker. We may not have enough money to donate to Ebola victims, but come wedding season and we will beg, borrow or steal, but make sure that every night is a Great Gatsby dream!

Apart from themed parties, other pre-wedding rituals and customs are the sagaai (engagement), tilak ceremony, haldi ceremony, sangeet and mehndi. The order of these ceremonies can vary depending on the family, but they generally take place the week prior to the wedding (in many cases the engagement is held a few weeks/months before the wedding). I am going to give you a sneak peek into what these ceremonies mean, how they are supposed to be conducted, and how—because we are severely damaged human beings—we have completely distorted them for the simple purpose of amusement!

Engagement Ceremony: Time to Pull Out the Big Guns!

The engagement or sagai is a grand affair that solidifies the formal contract between the two families. I know that the word 'contract' sounds very unromantic here, but technically that's what marriage is—a contract between two people, according to which they agree to live with each other and love each other forever (so then why a pre-nup?). The ring exchange between the couple is a stamp of confirmation. The bigger the diamond, the stronger the confirmation!

We love to make a big production out of everything and an engagement is living proof of that. It is the trailer to the 'wedding movie', but unlike the world of films, if this trailer is not a hit, there will be no wedding! Or worse, there will be a wedding followed by divorce! Or even worse, no divorce and lots of affairs!

Remember the song, '*Waah waah Ramji*' from *Hum Aapke Hain Kaun*, where Madhuri Dixit and Salman Khan happily sing away, in typical Sooraj Barjatya ish-style, for their respective siblings who just got engaged? I was twelve years old, when I watched this film and got seriously depressed when I realized that I would have to wait at least six years before I could legally get engaged. After watching those elaborate wedding functions on the big screen, women dressed up like goddesses, the exaggerated importance given to two people, all the handsome heroes running around singing songs for their leading ladies—I was hooked. So, the only thing I wanted to do was get engaged, and then, after a sufficient number of songs, get married into a family of 50,000 people, and wear red clothes and gold jewellery every day, while an imaginary Salman Khan showered me with compliments and gifts. Ironically, I am thirty-one years now and still unmarried. Something I totally blame on Bollywood! I mean where has it all disappeared—the romance, the sense of *janam-janam ka saath*, the unconditional love and support, and, the simplicity of it all. Now, we live in a generation where the maxim is—*affair karo, biwi se jhoot bolo, player bano, strip club jao*! Everybody wants to be bad, and somehow, good has become synonymous with boring.

In the past, the sacred sagai (engagement) ceremony was generally held at the bride's home, accompanied by music, dance and PG-rated fun. A priest would be present to bless the couple and conduct the affair by reciting some sacred mantras that no one understood. The two families would exchange gifts and blessings, after which the girl and boy exchanged rings in the presence of the elders and friends (*waah, kya sanskaar!*). Back then, girls were happy with a small diamond ring, as long as a certain something else was big enough (wink). Unfortunately, even that remained a mystery until the wedding, as every single hand was played in blind (just like for teen-patti) and one prayed to not end up with a joker! (These days, one doesn't even buy a car without first taking it for a test drive, let alone get married!)

This formal ring ceremony was to seal the deal, or to put it in sophisticated terminology—*game over, baby*! A few modern families would serve alcohol post the ring ceremony, but this was not the norm back then. It was the era of soft drinks and sherbat, with the men discreetly having a few drinks and the women busy gossiping about their daughters-in-law, comparing jewellery and bitching about the food. There were no DJs, no dance floor and no after party. Events ended at a civilized time—after all, there was no external stimulant to awaken the animal within.

Present-day engagement ceremonies are more or less the same, in terms of a ring exchange and blessings from the elders. But other than that, there is nothing about this function that even remotely resembles the original format of the past. Welcome to the age of *sharaab, kebab aur shebaab*!

There is a puja in the bride's home on the morning of the engagement, with a priest reciting mantras for the bride and groom and their life together. You see, we try and redeem ourselves before we resort to satanic behaviour during the actual engagement 'party' that takes place at night—a huge affair just like the wedding. Farmhouses and hotels with magnificent set-ups have replaced the home of the bride as the venue. An obnoxious amount of cash is spent doing up these spaces, so that the guests feel as though they have been transported to an exotic location abroad. Once the girl and boy exchange rings and the formalities are over, it's time to get wasted and get the party started! From *rab ne bana di jodi* to *pub ne bana di jodi*—we really have come a long way!

Most families these days organize professional entertainment for the guests—such as a live band, a skit or a performance by skilled dancers. It's fairly common for big Bollywood stars to make an appearance and glam up the proceedings for a couple of crores. Once the entertainment is over, the grand puppeteer of the party—the DJ—takes over. Unlike in the past, when the couple barely had any friends, these days, there are more youngsters than grown-ups at a party. The family is forced to take a back seat, while the friends take over, trying to re-create the Brazilian carnival inside the four walls of a hotel ballroom. Those close to the bride and groom feel that it's their duty to get everyone drunk and therefore, get busy forcing lethal shots down people's throats. In fact, these days, even the parents of the bride and groom get busy, making sure that no guest leaves the party unless he/she fails the breathalyzer test. This seems to be the mantra through most wedding functions, as the guests feel totally lost unless there's head-banging music, dancers from Ibiza and scary amounts of alcohol and other party uppers.

Tilak Ceremony: Alcohol-Free Zone

The tilak ceremony is one of the most important pre-wedding events, and regarded as very auspicious according to traditional Hindu customs. The main objective behind this ceremony is to punish our nearest and dearest—oops, I mean nurture the bond between the two families that are aligning through marriage. It is a very intimate affair with just close family members. KILL ME NOW.

Traditionally, only male family members attended this ceremony (the women lucked out), which would be held at either the groom's residence or at a temple. The ceremony would begin with a puja, during which both families prayed for the happiness of the new couple, or at least that's what we are told. After the puja, it was customary for the father of the bride to offer gifts to the groom's family, as if giving a daughter away was not enough! Ranging from fruits to clothes to sweets, the gifts were regarded as propitious. In exchange, the groom's father would send sugar, coconut, rice, clothes, jewellery and henna to the bride's family.

It was regarded as a sacred duty for the bride's family to smear a tilak on the forehead of the groom—this would guarantee that the groom would shoulder the responsibility of loving and taking care of his wife all her life. Damn! So this is the big secret! All you have to do is put a tilak on the groom's forehead, and bingo—all problems solved! Absolutely no divorces or separations ever!

The tilak ceremony remains one of the rare customs that has more or less remained untouched and untainted by demands of the present youth culture. It does NOT involve alcohol, music or any kind of disruptive behaviour, and therefore, the guest-list remains restricted. The only facet of this tradition that has evolved is the gifting. These days, the gifts exchanged include very costly clothes, jewellery, cars and plenty of hard cash. I know of families that have given close to a crore in cash to the groom as 'shagun'.

Funny, isn't it, how we have a billion of these pujas to secure the happiness and wellbeing of the couple, yet have the highest number of miserable men and women who would apply for divorce in a heartbeat? The truth is that no matter how many pujas you get done, how well your kundlis match, how much shagun you get, or how good your partner sounds on paper—if both of you are not compatible outside the bedroom, there will be trouble.

Nav Graha Puja: No Jokes

The priest performs this ceremony in both the bride's and groom's homes to offer prayers to the gods of the 'nine planets' and bestow blessings on the future couple. Once again, a private affair, with just immediate family members present. No jokes here. Come on, show some respect.

Haldi Ceremony: Let's Get Dirtyyyyy!

Welcome to the Indian version of the famous Tomatina festival that takes place in Spain every summer. The only difference is that during Tomatina, everyone throws tomatoes at each other, and during the haldi ceremony, everyone throws a yucky-looking yellow paste all over the bride and groom. Post-Tomatina, people are covered in red pulp; and after the haldi ceremony, the bride and groom are coated with dirty yellow pulp (pitthi), made of turmeric, chickpea flour and rose water, and supposedly good for the skin.

The haldi tradition has been going on for centuries, with friends and family applying the paste on the bride and groom to ensure their beautification before the actual ceremony. This is a daytime function with mostly close friends, family and—a recent addition—Café Patron. In some families, this ritual takes place on the morning of the wedding, whilst in others, it happens a few days before the big day. Either way, it's a lot of fun and everyone gets a chance to smother the couple with this potty-paste, until none of their skin is visible and they start looking like characters from *Planet of the Apes*.

The Sangeet Function : The Daddy of All Daddies!

There is something about tonight, something very special. The air is filled with the intoxicating fumes of hope and exhilaration. The fragrance of marigolds and carnations fused with the enchanting aroma of Chanel No 5. The blaze of hundreds of vintage chandeliers merged with next-level LED lighting. The afterglow of a million fairy lights (sparkling like diamonds in the sky) melded with the sparkle of countless precious stones and angelic attire. Here's the presence of unmatched beauty and perfection—enough to get anyone deliciously delirious.

As you walk into the most beautiful manmade haven created by some of the most talented decorators and wedding planners, you are instantly transported to a majestic era of kings and queens—where everything is flawless and surreal, just like a page out of a magazine named 'Fairytale Weddings of the Middle East'. One could get dizzy just looking around and taking it all in.

For those of you still wondering what the fuss is about, let me put you out of your misery. The sangeet or 'cocktail party' as many people call it, takes place two days before the wedding! That's right, just forty-eight hours to go! All those months of hectic planning, buying new clothes and jewellery, getting facials, dieting and committing to dance practice—and here we are—the moment of truth. Lights, camera, action! Brace yourselves, 'coz the show has just begun!

Traditionally, the sangeet was a women-only, alcohol-free function (yikes!) and took place at the bride's home. Just imagine a hundred women all dressed up, giving each other fake compliments, and driving the bride nuts with their expert marriage tips! 'Beti, make sure you are home every day when he comes back from work—because obviously his evening tea is more important than your career'; 'beta, never ask your husband probing questions'; '*arre baba, saare aadmi harami hote hain*. As long as he's not getting women home you're very lucky'; '*yeh love-shove kuch nahi hota, woh shopping le gayega. Aur kya chahiye?*'

Holy cow! Half these women probably had no idea that their tips would likely drive the poor groom into the arms of another woman—which is exactly what happened with their own husbands! Luckily, these women lived entire lifetimes in the bliss of ignorance, considering themselves pros after raising seventeen children. As women at the sangeet function were not meant to get intoxicated (and could not, in any case, without alcohol), they spent all day singing, dancing, and basically making the bride's life hell! The worst part: the bride did not have access to *even one drink* to numb her brains.

Fortunately, by the time my parents got married, this trend of dry, single-sex functions was history. By the 1980s and 1990s, sangeet functions included the moon, men and liquor. Having some harmless fun, while being slightly tipsy was not frowned upon. A small step for humanity—a huge leap for Punjabis. Hooray!

In the 1980s and 1990s, professional musicians would be called to play the traditional dholki along with other musical instruments, and sing popular Hindi film songs. Often, family members and close friends would sing along merrily, while also demonstrating their wrecked dancing skills! Many families would prepare a short performance for the clueless couple. These performances included a sentimental speech from either the mother or father of the bride/groom, a few short dances and some songs from the best singers in the family. The atmosphere would be a mixture of delight and despair, as the songs detailed the joys of starting a new life with the sadness of the bride leaving her family home. How sweet, right? Sanskaar 101.

The bride back then was made to dress down, with ordinary clothes and barely any make-up or jewellery, for all the functions and ceremonies that took place right before the wedding. This was so the bride would look stunning in comparison on the actual wedding day. Similarly, the décor was kept relatively simple—mostly flowers, rangoli and diyas, along with some spotlights for good photography. To sum it up, a sangeet party thirty years ago was simple, tasteful and fun with few complications, limited alcohol (no Café Patron back then) and an understated bride.

And now? Nothing is simple except for the parents' bank balance after the whole affair. Absurd chaos is the order of the day and, for the sangeet, the bride-to-be looks like a Christmas tree just flown in from Saks Fifth Avenue! The entire theory suggesting the bride should look simple before the wedding has gone out the window, with top A-list designers coming up with new bridal couture designs every year. The bride's father will sell his kidney if he has to, but will get his daughter the most expensive designer clothes for her wedding. The trend now is to build up the look until the wedding day. So, we start with a ₹5,00,000 outfit and keep ascending until the D-day, with the wedding lehenga anything between ₹10,00,000 to ₹50,00,000.

The same formula is followed for the jewellery (lucky jewellers), so we start with delicate understated pearl and diamond sets (open houses) and then gradually go up the ladder with bigger and blingier looking diamonds, rubies, emeralds, pearls, polki, kundan—the list is endless. I know of brides who wear jewellery worth ₹1,00,00,000 or more on the day of the wedding. Whoa! I want to get my hands on some of that, but unfortunately, my father is an honest lawyer, who pays way too much tax—so, I'm guessing not in this lifetime! God knows that I have tried my best to convince him to leave law and join politics—at least, until he makes enough black money to sponsor my dream wedding in Istanbul. But sadly, my father is a saint and probably one of the last men on earth who values his integrity more than entertaining a thousand people in Turkey and buying his daughter big diamonds (sad face)!

Exquisite attire is not just the bride's right—these days the guests, too, dress to impress. It's kind of like Oktoberfest, but with really expensive clothes, diamond sets that cost more than a house in Beverly Hills, a concert stage with fancy LED screens, the latest laser lights and international DJs flown in from different parts of the world. This is not a party; it's a parade—a red carpet parade, a work of art, a masterpiece.

These days the sangeet function is given more importance than the wedding itself. It has become the star of the wedding with the maximum number of attendees—at least a thousand people. In fact, many social acquaintances are invited *only* for this function. There are multiple bars serving the best of the best alcohol, with champagne flowing like water, and shots being consumed like chilled lemonade on a hot day.

This is also the night of the BIG performance, for which the friends and family have worked hard (remember the dance practice sessions?). This part of the evening usually starts at around 10.30 or 11.00 p.m. (earlier for destination weddings) and can go on for forty-five minutes. The format varies from family to family, but the main elements remain the same. Two or more emcees do the talking and entertain the guests. Along with this, there are at least forty to fifty people dancing (including the bride and groom) to the latest Bollywood hit songs. What started off as a casual fun performance has now become a full-blown Broadway extravaganza with lots of glitter and glamour. Be it specialized sound effects and lighting, or top of the line special effects, we have it all.

The performance is literally what gets the party started. This show is very special for the bride and groom, as they are the centre of attention and every word said is about them—highlighting either their virtues or vices. This is also a great way for single girls to display their 'moves' and flaunt their pretty faces to lure unsuspecting single men (prey). It's a well-known fact that wedding functions (especially the sangeet) are the best way to find a partner.

Once the performances are over, the real show begins. The DJ is the star of the night, without whom the party would be a complete disaster. Imagine a bunch of drunk people without music trying to channel their excessive energy through conversation! Frankly, I would rather sit at home and watch Arnab's show on *Times Now* if that's the kind of evening I'm looking for. Intoxicated people *need* loud music with complex electronic beats to get them in the mood.

Thanks to the DJ, by 2 a.m., the dance floor is completely packed with drunk uncles, super-hot aunties and youngsters who can't stand straight. Even people who hate each other in real life are seen dancing away, shaking their bums in unison, proving to themselves what good dancers they are. This is a deadly combination of music, alcohol and a thousand people passionate about partying all night—and is the result of modern cinema with talented directors like Zoya Akhtar (my favourite) and Homi Adajania, who are changing the landscape of Indian cinema and what it represents. Where once girls from 'good' families were forbidden from going even near alcohol, these days brides can't take their pheras without first polishing off at least two bottles of champagne and a joint. When we see all the top heroines going nuts on the big screen, it makes us feel less guilty doing it ourselves!

A sangeet can go on until 6 a.m., with approximately 30 per cent of the guests willing to party even longer. Too wired to go back home and too sozzled to know what's going on, they hang around until the staff starts packing things up. How these people make it for the mehndi function the same afternoon is beyond me

I usually miss the mehndi—I mean, can you imagine sleeping at 6 a.m., and making it for the next function by 1 p.m.? Nonetheless, this is something I am working on currently.

Mehndi Function: The Sundowner to Beat All Sundowners!

There is the grey shadow of a hangover lurking in the air. Guests walk in wearing sunglasses to hide their bloodshot eyes, carrying tiny bottles of water and strips of Aspirin. Those who have spent the morning vomiting are quietly sitting and and enjoying the calm before the storm. The rest are waiting in line for the next available washroom, so that they can download the remaining alcohol from the night before. For the first time in eight chapters, the youngsters are actually eating food. This is probably the only wedding function where the bar is nearly empty (out of choice) for the first couple of hours. It's understandable, as these are the people who were the last ones to leave the sangeet in the wee hours of the morning. Considering they only managed to squeeze in a few hours of sleep, before they had to wake up, get dressed and be on time for the next function, we cut them some slack. After all, we don't want people falling sick right before the big day.

If the sangeet is the star of the wedding, then the mehndi is definitely the soul—usually taking place twenty-four hours before D-day. Not a single Indian bride has ever got married without getting embellished with beautiful, intricate mehndi designs that have now gained popularity all over the world. Mehndi, or henna as it is popularly known, is a paste derived from the Henna tree that is decoratively applied to the bride's hands, arms and feet. Popular lore states that the darker the bride's mehndi turns out, the more her new husband and mother-in-law will love her. That makes so much sense because clearly the henna colour has nothing to do with the quality of the leaves, but instead depends on the quality of love offered by two unpredictable human beings. We might be lagging when it comes to education and birth control; but when it concerns logic, we are the champions!

Traditionally, mehndi was a private function, held at the bride's home and attended largely by women, immediate family members and close friends of the bride.

Once again, the women sang and danced to traditional songs about marriage and unions (for the millionth time. I swear to god, if I have to write the words 'singing', 'dancing' and 'women' once more, I will shoot myself.) The mother of the bride or a close relative would apply the symbolic first mehndi marks, after which a professional mehndi artist would continue the application, with traditional designs containing auspicious symbols. The mehndi artist would write the groom's name somewhere in the midst of the mehndi design, which the groom would have to find as part of post-wedding rituals. Why did this happen? I have no clue! But I do know that once the mehndi was applied, the bride couldn't leave her home until the wedding.

While the bride was busy getting ready for the joys of matrimony, the female guests too, were busy getting their own hands and feet beautified by some of the most skilled henna artists.

We Indians, as ardent lovers of beauty and elegance (throw in a good measure of abhorrent monkey behaviour), have gone on to amend the mehndi ceremony, too. To begin with, we now have a range of henna styles that did not exist in the past—Arabic, Rajasthani, crystal, tattoo mehndi. Young women mostly like to experiment with modern mehndi designs, showing a marked preference for Arabic or crystal mehndi. Truly, we will do anything to defy our ancestors and rub their conservative noses to the ground, in a bid to senselessly rebel.

Over the years, the mehndi function has become one of the most colourful and among the liveliest wedding affairs, with gorgeous, bright outfits, vibrant music and enthusiastic dance moves. This is the only wedding function where the bride is not showered with diamonds and instead is seen in delicate jewellery made out of pretty flowers. In fact, it is the only time you can actually see what the bride looks like! The same holds true for the guests and it's refreshing to actually see people properly, without layers and layers of make-up and enough ornaments to give the king of Saudi a huge complex.

Once the guests have successfully nursed their hangovers, off come the sunglasses and once again, the balance of power is restored. The dholki guys are back with a bang and there are not more than a handful of people who are able to resist the temptation of getting jiggy with them. It's incredible to see the change in people—struggling to sit up straight a few hours earlier and now bouncing off walls with a newfound energy. The memories of the previous night/morning fade away, as newer memories that are more exciting are created.

Once the application of mehndi is complete, the bride, too, joins all the madness. Unlike the past, when a bride was meant to lie low and remain a fly on the wall watching everyone else have fun, these days the bride and groom are as much a part of the mehndi shenanigans as the other guests, downing Café Patron shots and consuming lethal quantities of Kingfisher Premium. My sister was actually asked to get off the speaker (she thought it was kept there for people to get on and dance) by the hotel staff, who were clearly horrified by this barbaric display of fun.

This is yet another function that has evolved from a small, private, mostly women, no alcohol affair, to an all-day sundowner with at least five hundred people, and lots of *shor, sharaba, aur sharab*. Songs such as *'Mehndi laga ke rakhna'* and *'Mere haathon mein nau nau chudiyan hai'* have been kicked out by new tracks from Avicii and Fatboy Slim. Beach house remixes and the best of Tomorrowland have replaced Bollywood songs as the primary form of entertainment. My sister's mehndi function (in Goa) is the best example of what we have turned the mehndi function into—a day party at the Blue Marlin beach club in Ibiza! Guests in their best beachwear, sipping their beers and bobbing their heads up and down to the beats of 'Eat, sleep, rave, repeat', with the drop-dead gorgeous backdrop of the ocean. Sun, sand and sangria—what more can one ask for?

The wedding planners leave no stone unturned, with creativity oozing out of every corner of the venue. There are stalls filled with stunning multicoloured bangles and bindis of all shapes and sizes, and women there to help the guests pick out their favourite ones. I have seen lovely Indian scarves and saris with beautiful intricate embroidery and workmanship being distributed to the bride's close friends and family. There are astrologers with their parrots and Tarot card readers with their decks, telling the single girls that they will soon find their prince charming. Freshly prepared hot street food of every type available in India is served to the guests. As the day progresses into the night, the party turns from a chilled-out sundowner into a full-blown carnival. Combine the energy bestowed by the Café Patron with the trippy beats of the DJ and dholwaalas, and we have got ourselves a mini festival going.

🔽

Pre-wedding functions get people closer and create a wonderful fun-filled atmosphere before the wedding. You really need to attend one of these to know what I am talking about. Sure, the slew of activities may sound intimidating and tiring, but when you see the bride and groom take the plunge into matrimony, while trying to remember what the hell happened the night before—it makes it all worth it!

The last thirty years have seen astounding

advancement in the Indian wedding industry. From home to hotel, roses to cruises, chai to champagne and from a big dil to a big bill—we have literally re-invented the entire wedding landscape. The bride is no longer shy, the groom no longer tense (*arre, mummy-pappa hai na tension lene ke liye*) and the mothers-in-law too busy shopping and grooming themselves to interfere in the lives of their kids and piss them off daily.

In fact, people are so engrossed with their own lives that no one even has the time to share feelings and thoughts with one another, despite living under the same roof. Kids hear about their parents' whereabouts from random strangers, and parents follow their children's lives on Facebook and Instagram.

On that note, I proudly announce the end of contagious pre-wedding fever that makes a victim of everyone—from five-year-olds to those touching ninety-five.

With all the customs, traditions and liver function tests out of the way, we finally get to the big day that we have all been eagerly waiting for. Nowhere else in the whole wide world are weddings given the kind of importance they are in India. If you can survive this rollercoaster of merriment, then you are what we call a true trooper! RESPECT.

The Wedding: Abhi Toh Party Shuru Hui Hai

First, congratulations to my readers, fellow Indians, and every bride and groom who ever got married. You have all made it to this day in one piece, and shall live to tell the tale, just like me! Seriously, making it to the final wedding day—without any serious injuries or a liver transplant, and with all body parts working—is no joke! After the last eight chapters, you might well be asking yourselves a few valid questions: Does this damn thing ever end? How much can one expect from a human being?

Millions of functions, rituals, customs and holidays, we have done it all! Dazzling décor, an elaborate sumptuous spread, a live band, a DJ, Bollywood stars, multiple bars, fireworks, an after party—we have not left any stone unturned, any source untapped! We have literally lived through every moment that the bride and groom experience, from the time of the proposal right until NOW—the D-day! Every single word that I have written has been leading up to this chapter. This is it, the last day of this never-ending circus, the final episode of the wedding series, an end with a new beginning! Time to leave the airport lounge and board the flight to 'destination unknown'!

Indian weddings are all about highlighting beliefs, token symbolism and traditions, bringing families and friends together, and making a huge contribution towards the economy. There are a gazillion people, who run their homes, thanks to this booming industry. Caterers, bootleggers, tentwaalas, lightwaalas, soundwaalas, DJs, phoolwaalas, mehndiwaalis, beauticians, fashion designers and jewellers—they would all be out of business, if there were no big fat Indian weddings.

The guest list for a big Indian wedding has at least a thousand names on it, and when I say thousand, I mean *two* thousand! Every single person that you, your parents, your grandparents, your siblings, your cousins and your friends have met in their lifetimes, is invited. The only exception is a destination wedding—in which case the guest list includes only five hundred people. I know that anyone who has not been brought up in India is probably thinking, 'Five hundred! Holy Cow!' But that's just how we operate. We love people, period. Once again, thank you Bollywood.

✘

The elaborate Indian wedding has been a popular theme in Bollywood since the 1990s (*Hum Saath Saath Hain*). In such films, it didn't matter whether weddings were arranged or love matches, whether they made sense or not, as long as they were big budget and full of bling. With a song, every two minutes, the bride and groom were, at any point, in the hallowed presence of at least thirty immediate family members (mummy, papa, bhaiya, bhabhi, didi, jeeju, tauji, taiji, chacha, chachi, mama, mami, bua, phoopha, mausi, massar...). These chaps loved each other to bits. They had dinner together every night, prayed together every morning, sang together in happiness and sorrow, and gave each other expensive gifts regularly. Back then, joint families were the 'in' thing and everyone wanted to be a part of this massive 'parivaar' that did everything together including taking a dump! (A huge contrast to present times, where the definition of a joint family is a family that smokes pot together: *Arre, Papa joint pass karu che!*)

Illustration © Fiza Khan

SONAL AND ROHITS WEDDING ITINERARY

Thank you for joining us to celebrate the union of two of the most amazing people we know, Sonal Shah and Rohit Singh. in case of any queries or issues, please contact : KumKum (bride's sister) +91 9734562711 or Varun (Groom's uncle) +91 8965466632

Sunday 17/1/16	11:00 AM	Welcome to New Delhi!!!
	11:30 AM	Drop off to your hotel
	11:30 - 3:30	Rest, eat, relax : the hotel has a great lunch buffet!
	3:30 PM	Groom's home for dance practice (our car's on call at reception)
	7:00 PM on	Dinner / drinks at the groom (Rohit Singh's) home
Monday 18/1/16	12:00 noon	Lunch at Rohit's
	2:00 - 5:00	Dance practice!!!!
	5:00-7:00	Puja ceremony (bring adequate head covering for this please)
	7:00- 10:00	Dinner at Rimpy Bua's (drivers / car's on call)
	10:00 PM on	After party at Dolly and Varun's home
Tuesday 19/1/16	12:00 noon	sight seeing / shopping (car's / driver's are on call at the reception
	3:00-6:00	Dance practice!!!!
	6:00-8:00	back to the hotel to freshen up and get ready
	8:00-10:00	Dholki (save your singing voice for this!)
	10:00 PM on	Dinner / drinks at Dhir Tau-Jee's house
Wednesday 20/1/16	12:00 noon	Brunch at Sonal's (bride to be!) house
	3:00-5:00	Puja (again please bring appropriate head covering)
	5:00-6:00	Mata ki chawki
	6:00-8:00	Dance practice!!!
	8:00-10:00	Back to the hotel to freshen up (driver's on call!)
	10:00 PM on	Dholki at Sonal's house
Thursday 21/1/16	12:00 noon	Lunch at Rohit's
	3:00- 4:00	Tilak ceremony (at residence only)
	4:00-7:00	Dance practice!!
	7:00-8:00	hotel to freshen up (driver's on call!)
	8:00 PM on	Mama Bhat dinner at Jai mama's farm and after party

SONAL AND ROHITS WEDDING ITINERARY

Thank you for joining us to celebrate the union of two of the most amazing people we know, Sonal Shah and Rohit Singh. in case of any queries or issues, please contact : KumKum (bride's sister) +91 9734562711 or Varun (Groom's uncle) +91 8965466632

Friday 22/1/16	12:00 noon	Puja at Groom's house (please bring appropriate head covering)
	1:00-3:00	Lunch at Rohit's house
	3:00-6:00	Final dance practice!
	6:00-7:00	hotel to freshen up (driver's on call!)
	8:00PM-7:00AM	Sangeet night !!!! ALL - NIGHT - LONG
Saturday 3/1/16	1:00-6:00	Mehendi ceremony at Singhania Farm's
	6:00-8:00	hotel to freshen up (driver's on call!)
	8:00 PM on	Dinner at Malika Singh's house (Rohit's sister)
Sunday /1/16	**WEDDING DAY!!!!!**	
	12:00 noon	Brunch at Rohit's house
	2:00-3:00	Sehra bandi
	3:00-4:00	Assembly of the baraat
	4:00-7:00	Baraat
	7:00-8:00	Milnee
	8:00-8:30	Jai Mala
	8:30-11:00	Phera's
	11:00-1:00	Dinner
	1:00 AM on	Party followed by After party
day /16	All day	Appollo hospital!!!!

just joking! however if you do need any assistance please feel free to contact the following numbers :

Spa : 011 23456743 / 011 245678990
Salon: 011 254678342
medical : 011 2345 88765
Cab with driver : 011 22224534 / 011 24456767
Please feel free to contact KumKum or Varun for any assistance!

Thank you!!

Illustration © Fiza Khan

MALHOTRA & YADAV

To,
Mr arvind malhotra, CEO

From,
Rohan Singh, head of sales

Subject: letter of resignation 12 / 03 / 2015

Dear sir,

I would like to thank you for giving me the opportunity to work and grow with a company as fine as Malhotra & Yadav, however I feel that I will no longer be able to maintain the standards of excellence expected from your employees.

Therefore with much respect I would like you to treat this letter as my official note of resignation, the reason being that in the coming few months I have no less than seven wedding's to attend. As you may well be aware, to attend in full participation even one wedding along with its meteor trail of sangeet's, youngster's and various other events, is no small feat requiring full allotment of time. To attend seven would be impossible to do with a full time job.

I hope you will understand my predicament, and I look forward to opening a dialogue with you early next year with the prospect of returning to Malhotra & Yadav as a full time employee.

Sincerely

Rohan Singh

Rohan Singh

to

Mr Malhotra

Illustration © Fiza Khan

Illustration © Fiza Khan

Illustration © Fiza Khan

Illustration © Fiza Khan

What these movies lacked in terms of a good story line was more than made up for with approximately three million characters. This was the era of strong family values, where both the boy and girl were shy and conservative, had no friends to give them any kind of perspective (understandable, when you have such a large family), and fell in love with each other faster than it takes my MAC Pro to restart. Not only did they find their soulmates in under a minute, they also knew that they were meant to be with each other for the next seven lifetimes (*janam janam ka saath*). Wow! I find it hard to commit to seven months with a guy, let alone seven lifetimes. Either, we are lazy now, or these people were crazy back then.

All the movies in what I call the 'marriage genre' had a similar story line and jumped from one wedding function to another, all highlighting the importance of family, love and drama. From the roka to sagai, from sagai to sangeet, from sangeet to mehndi, from mehndi to wedding, from wedding to godh bharai—the list never ended. It seems as if the entire purpose of all human existence was marriage and everything related to it. The women sat at home and cooked maa ki dal, while the men of the house were busy earning money to sponsor expensive Kanjeevaram sarees and a roomful of toys for a kid that was yet to be born. Roles were clearly divided and there was absolutely no question of re-assigning duties.

Interestingly, one can see the transfer of such wedding fever from reel life to real life. The 1990s hit us hard, with the glorified villains being replaced by god-fearing Mummyji and Papaji; college picnics being replaced by family picnics; and Amrish Puri abandoning his psycho-rapist avatar to become father of the year! Even Shakti Kapoor stopped being the bad guy and started preferring comic roles, something that shook me to the core. This transformation in the film industry sparked a desire in people to believe that they, too, could be a part of the family fantasy created by filmmakers. Movies like *Dilwale Dulhania Le Jayenge* gave birth to the ultimate mummy-papa-bua-dadi characters—and people wished to assume their identities during weddings. All the mummyjis wanted to become their daughter's best friend; all the papajis enrolled for a foreign visa and a crash course in 'Sanskaar 101'; and every young girl and boy yearned to become Simran and Raj. It was an era of love, and love truly did conquer all.

Even though the 1990s started the trend of lots of colour, music, dance and functions, it was still the age of sobriety and values. The bride and groom were the centre of attention and everything from the entertainment to the hospitality was highly personal. Parents from both sides personally attended to all the guests, making sure they were well fed and looked after. In most cases, the wedding took place at the bride's home, with the father, uncles and brothers all teary eyed at the thought of finally giving away their beautiful princess.

The gorgeous bride, dressed up in her *laal shaadi ka joda*, adorned with her grandmother's antique gold jewellery, would wait for the groom, who arrived on a white mare, like a knight-in-shining-amour, and swept her off her feet (umm...not really!). The groom would reach the wedding venue, along with his family and friends, who would be singing and dancing in a procession, with the dhol and bandwaalas playing typical wedding tunes in the background: *'Aaj mere yaar ki shaadi hai'*. This is what we call a baraat and the original concept was quite simple. This was how the boy's family showed their excitement about the wedding, as well as their eagerness to take away the bride. Back then, this pre-wedding celebration lasted for about thirty minutes. There was no alcohol, as it was considered inauspicious to drink before or during wedding rituals.

After the baraat, everyone would be in a festive mood, and the bride and groom would take blessings from all the elders present, eagerly awaiting the mahurat, so they could take their vows. It was all very dharmic and cute. There were no delays or disturbances and people were very well behaved.

↙

Weddings today seem to have taken a 180-degree turn, and I can safely say that a wedding in 2015 has only a slight resemblance to a wedding in 1992.

For one, the baraat is an event in itself. Gone are the days of liquor-free existence. Now it doesn't matter what the occasion—puja or no puja, pheras or no pheras, there will be alcohol, and not just alcohol, but ALL the alcohol available under the sun. Welcome to the era of '*band baja baraat, hum peeyengey saari raat!*'

So what does a baraat look like these days? I hope you are sitting down because what I am about to share with you is going to be hard to believe—just like all the Café Patron consumed during this three-hour MDMA-fuelled experience that we call a baraat! The days of '*Aaj mere yaar ki shaadi hai*' are SO over. Now we have songs like, '*Bottlein khulwaado*', '*Bhootni ke*', '*Shaadi hai barbaadi*', and '*Talli hua, talli hua*'. The concept of a baraat has been completely redefined (just like all the other aspects of a wedding) and remoulded. If I were to give you a comparison, then a baraat twenty years ago was like having cutting chai with greasy pakodas. Now it's a magnum bottle of Dom Pérignon—and throw in a few bottles of Beluga and some Russian caviar for good measure.

These days grooms have many options for their baraat 'ride'. The white mare has been reduced to a nightmare, with other, much fancier choices available such as chariots and vintage cars. These are popular, as baraats go on for three to four hours, and the groom is much more comfortable in a proper seat, rather than fidgeting on a mare, trying to undo his wedgie under all that heavy clothing.

This is one day when it's hard to distinguish between the bride and groom, as both are burdened with heavy clothes and even heavier jewellery. The groom is seen wearing layers and layers of emeralds and pearls, a funny head contraption, holding a sword in one hand and a glass of scotch in the other. *Style hai bhai*, and I don't care what anyone else thinks, but a last drink as a bachelor *toh banta hai*.

Even though, traditionally, it was taboo to drink right before the wedding, these days it's impossible to stay sober during a baraat, as a mobile bar moves along with the procession, offering all sorts of shots and other hard liquor. To further aid the process, drinks are also pre-made in Bisleri bottles, half-liquor and half-water. These bottles are passed on to all the baraatis and one family member/friend is given the responsibility of making sure that everyone is absolutely shattered by the time the procession reaches the final venue. Another van that slowly follows the baraat has fancy toilets, in the likely event that the baraatis need to download some of the liquid that they are consuming at a very rapid pace. A third vehicle follows with the DJ spinning rocking summer tracks from Tomorrowland, giving the bandwaalas some serious competition. Clearly, what started as a brief fun-filled experience in anticipation of the wedding has turned into a large-scale roadside festival with liquor, snacks, toilets, bandwaalas, dholwaalas, DJs—and a billion people. The wedding has become the obstacle that comes in the way of this magical experience and people get very aggressive while trying to prevent the baraat from ending.

It is essential for the modern-day baraat to be at least two hours late. In fact, unlike in the boring past, when it was considered inauspicious for the groom to arrive after the 'shubh mahurat', these days it's considered inauspicious for the groom to reach on time. *Waheguru, Waheguru, kya zamaana aa gaya hai*! A groom, who does not have at least a hundred crazy people in his baraat and who reaches the wedding venue on time, is considered a loser. The friends and family will go to any extent to make sure that the baraat is delayed as much as possible. The girl's parents have to literally threaten cancelling the wedding, before the groom's side agrees to end the mad parade and let the groom get married in peace. I have actually been witness to conversations where people say things like, 'The baraat only lasted two hours, yaar. And there was no Café Patron! Can you imagine? The time for the pheras was 8 p.m. and we reached by 8.30 p.m.! How lame, na! What a loser!'

I recently attended a close friend's wedding, where the baraat continued for an hour-and-a-half, after the groom sneakily ran into the venue for fear of upsetting the bride and her parents. It was epic. No one really cared that the groom was no longer a part of the baraat; we were having such a good time that we overlooked this minor detail. Finally, we had to stop as the bride's mother started sending out some serious threats and we realized that this wedding would not start until we stopped. Argh...these party-poopers!

While the groom and his people are busy remapping all boundaries, the modern-day bride is not far behind. In the past, brides were ready before time, quietly waiting for the baraat to arrive, nervously anticipating the future, and starving to death (traditionally, the bride and groom fasted until the wedding ceremony). There were cousins and a few girlfriends present for the sole purpose of entertaining the bride, but it was pretty boring and demanding, waiting on an empty stomach with fifty kilograms of clothing and jewellery. Alcohol was completely out of the question, as this was the chai-coffee generation.

Luckily, for women, things have completely turned around. The bride of 2015 knows that the baraat is not coming any time soon, so she takes her own sweet time getting dressed, in what has now become at least a three-hour process. There is an entourage of make-up artists and hairstylists working on the bride, so that she looks perfectly airbrushed, polished and stunning, just like a top Bollywood actress. When my sister got married in Goa, we had to go through this process every day for three days. It wasn't harrowing at all, as we hooked up brilliant speakers with sensational beach house tracks playing in the background, and everyone (including the make-up and hair guys) happily sipped on their beers while at work, and enjoyed the lovely view of the ocean that we were blessed with, thanks to our villa. It was amaze-balls! In fact, my sister was having such a good time getting dressed, she didn't realize that she was over an hour late, and the baraat had to do a U-turn, dance some more and come back later! But cases like this are extremely rare and my family is not what you would call 'normal'.

In more normal families, once the bride is ready, it's time to pop some champagne and get one's groove on (yeah, that's our definition of normal!). Can you come up with a better way to wait for the groom? NO! So now, the fully decked bride sits in her bridal suite or whichever fancy suite her parents booked her in, gulping down champagne, one glass after another, while her friends keep her calm and distracted. There are some serious last-minute jitters and the bride-to-be starts questioning her decision to get married. At this point, the parents start sending gentle reminders to the baraat, urging them to hurry up before the bride gets too drunk and decides she is better off without the moron groom (oh, subtle!).

Then begins the never-ending tug-of-war. The bride's family is trying their best to end the baraat and get the show off the road. The groom and his friends absolutely refuse to listen to any reasoning, prolonging the baraat for as long as they physically can. I have seen my friends go to bizarre lengths to prevent the mare/vintage car/chariot from moving ahead, including lying down flat on the road in front of the vehicle, shouting, '*Mere upar se chadda ke lekar jaa!*' (*Waah, waah, waah,* whoever says India is a backward country, really needs to re-examine the evidence. I mean, look at us. We might not know how to potty-train our kids, but give us some liquor and we can conquer the world.)

Once the baraat ends, after much deliberation, it's finally time to do the deed that has been the whole point behind everything that has taken place over the past year! All the baraatis line up outside the wedding venue (totally shit-faced) while the bride's family executes an elaborate welcome for the groom. This is called vara satkaarah—the ceremony where the bride's mother welcomes the groom by applying a tilak and rice grains on his forehead. This is officially when the fun begins. The groom is seated on a special chair, where the bride's brother or relative washes the groom's feet (oh, kinky!). This is considered a sign of respect, but according to me, it is just a strategic move to get the groom to take his shoes off so that they can be stolen.

This is another interesting tradition that we have been blessed with as part of our elaborate heritage— and it involves stealing. We are not unlike the Italians when it comes to being totally gangsta! Not only do we steal the groom's shoes, we also demand a huge sum of cash in return for the shoes. I have often wondered why this happens, but have never been bothered enough to investigate. Unless it's my own brother out there getting married, I don't really care. They can steal shoes, jewellery, bags, cars or whatever they like.

After feet cleansing/shoe stealing comes the exchange of garlands (between the bride and groom), or as we call it, jaimala. This is a gesture of acceptance of one another and a pledge to respect each other (yeah baby, I only made you wait for three hours, see how much I respect you!). While this entire scene is unfolding, the friends are by the bar getting even more shit-faced. I mean come on; you can't get people drunk and then suddenly expect them to behave seriously and get sanskaari. We are no longer on the sets of Rajshri Productions. This is Boys Gone Wild Pvt Ltd, where even the groom is drunk, but has to pretend to be sober or else the panditji will throw a fit.

Are you thinking what I am thinking? What the fuck

is going on here? Why is everyone so drunk and why is no one taking anything seriously? The poor bride's parents are in a state of shock (and slightly drunk), the groom's parents are secretly embarrassed (and slightly drunk), wishing the earth would just suck them in The bride is livid and partly drunk due to the long wait, the groom and his friends are all wasted. In the meantime, the panditji, who I am pretty sure smoked a fatty before coming, thinks he is on a talk show, and is doing sound checks on the mic. At some level, I think it's hilarious, like a slapstick comedy, where everything is meant to be funny and nothing is a source of concern.

Now, the father of the bride welcomes the allegedly sober groom to the vivah mandap. While the groom is wondering where the hell his friends have disappeared, the priest lights up the holy fire and starts chanting Vedic verses signifying the start of the wedding. After some time, the bride's sister or the sister-in-law guides the bride to the vivah mandap, where she is seated next to the confused groom, all dressed up in her thirty-lakh-ka-lehenga and jewellery worth at least a crore (*chotti baat*).

The bride and groom then start repeating verses as directed by the priest. The groom's life flashes before his eyes and he silently says goodbye to his existence as a bachelor. The bride's credit cards and shopping bills flash before her eyes, bringing tears of sadness and a fear of the unknown—it is so unsettling not knowing which credit cards and what credit limits await you in the future; Papa might just have to come to the rescue. Unlike the 1970s and 1980s, papas of today are too good, yaar. They will fight the world for you and make sure that there's not even a scratch on your Bentley and Berkin collection.

We then move on to the kanyaadaan, which refers to the ceremony where one officially gives away the daughter in marriage. During this ritual, the father places the bride's left hand in the groom's right hand. The groom promises the bride's father (while trying not to vomit) that he shall protect her and be with her in the good and bad times. Well, or at least, until he finds someone with a slimmer waistline and bigger boobs! The groom then hesitantly accepts the bride as his awfully—oops, I mean, *lawfully*— wedded wife, a ritual we call paani graham.

Finally, we move on to mangal pheras, during which, the bride and the groom go around the sacred fire seven times. Each phera symbolizes a marriage vow (wow) and it is also believed that the seven pheras mark their union for seven births. For the first four pheras, the groom leads the bride and for the next three pheras, the bride leads the groom. I have no idea why this happens, but I have explained the sacred seven vows below, what they mean and how they are interpreted these days. Bazinga!

1. Provision and Nourishment [4]

Groom: You will offer me food and be helpful in every way. I will cherish you and provide for the welfare and happiness of you and our children.
Interpretation: You are a glorified maid! I will take you for granted and crib about all the money you spend on yourself and the brats!

Bride: I am responsible for the home and all household responsibilities.
Interpretation: Go screw yourself. I am now entitled to half your wealth. Don't mess with me, you coward.

2. Strength

Groom: Together we will protect our house and children.
Interpretation: I have been reduced to a damn babysitter! If I waste all my time protecting you fools, who the hell is going to make money?

Bride: I will be by your side as your courage and strength.

---

4. For the literal readings, see 'Seven Vows', *Cultural India*, in <http://www.culturalindia.net/weddings/wedding-traditions/seven-vows.html>, accessed on 19 June 2015.

I will rejoice in your happiness. In return, you will love me exclusively.

Interpretation: You were a complete loser before I married you; you should be glad my presence earned you a promotion. You had better love me the way I want you to—or else, talk to my super-expensive lawyers, who, by the way, you will pay for!

3. *Prosperity*

Groom: May we grow wealthy and prosperous and strive for the education of our children. May our children live long.

Interpretation: Stop wasting my hard-earned money on useless nonsense! We need to save for our hopeless kids or else they will be on the road by the time you are done collecting your Berkins!

Bride: I will love you solely for the rest of my life, as you are my husband. Every other man in my life will be secondary. I vow to remain chaste.

Interpretation: My love is conditional, do you understand? If you piss me off, I am going to bang every single man in sight!

4. *Family*

Groom: You have brought sacredness into my life, and have completed me. May we be blessed with noble and obedient children.
Interpretation: You give me tension, if I fail to give you attention! You have brought ulcers into my life. The kids will hate me and I hate you.

Bride: I will shower you with joy, from head to toe. I will strive to please you in every way I can.
Interpretation: I will show you what tension is, you ungrateful piece of shit! First, learn how to please a woman, you clueless frog!

5. Friendship

Groom: You are my best friend, and staunchest well-wisher. You have come into my life, enriching it. God bless you.
Interpretation: You are milking me dry! The devil has sent you into my life to sabotage my happiness. Satan, please take her back.

Bride: I promise to love and cherish you for as long as I live. Your happiness is my happiness, and your sorrow is my sorrow. I will trust and honour you, and will strive to fulfill all your wishes.

Interpretation: I promise to be a pain in the ass for as long as I live. Your wallet is my wallet, and your mother is a witch!

6. Happiness

Groom: May you be filled with joy and peace.
Interpretation: Do what you like, just let me live in peace!

Bride: I will always be by your side.
Interpretation: Finally, you are developing a sense of humour, you senseless moron! Anyway, now you're stuck with me. All the best to you!

7. Love

Groom: We are now husband and wife, and are one. You are mine and I am yours for eternity.
Interpretation: I want to kill myself.

Bride: As god is my witness, I am now your wife. We will love, honour and cherish each other forever.
Interpretation: No! Don't kill yourself! As your wife, I am entitled to treat myself to this pleasure!

I admit that, at one level, my interpretations are highly exaggerated, but they are also based on reality and there is a strong element of truth in each one of them. Many couples very conveniently forget their marriage vows and start behaving like Dracula's descendants, thirsty for blood, willing to go to any extent for it. If vows are not routinely misinterpreted, then why on earth are so many people getting divorced these days? Do people forget their vows or does the love just go out of the window? I guess, I will have to wait until I get married to find out. How exciting! I look forward to it.

Coming back to the last leg of the race, once the seven pheras are completed, the newlywed couple seeks blessings from the elders in both the families. I am not sure how this is done in the West, but in India, touching the feet of those older is a sign of respect and proof of good sanskaars. So, during a wedding, where hundreds of people are old, and feet need to be touched, I feel very sorry for the bride and groom. Maybe this is the reason couples end their gym memberships before getting married—they know they will be getting enough exercise, literally bending over every chance they get.

Once all the blessings have been acquired, it's time for the bride and groom to finally feed each other a morsel of food and some delicious mithai. Sweets are essential at this point, because we believe that it's auspicious to start anything new by sweetening our palate.

The groom now applies a small dot of vermillion

(sindoor), a purified form of cinnabar, to the bride's forehead and welcomes her as his partner for life. Remember the line, '*Ek chutki sindoor ki keemat tum kya jano, Ramesh babu*' from the movie *Om Shanti Om*? Yeah, that's the stuff I am talking about. No Indian bride is complete without a pinch of this running down her parting.

And on that note, I now pronounce the bride and groom husband and wife. Hurrah! It is finally done. The bride and groom are now legally blond (ha!)—I mean, bound! Both sets of parents are now samdhis, and everyone goes a bit crazy hugging and kissing each other. It's actually a very emotionally charged moment with tears welling up in everyone's eyes. Well, the tears are partly due to fatigue and partly due to the sanctity of the moment— but mostly on account of high intoxication.

While all this drama is taking place, the little sisters of the bride are trying to strike a deal with their new jeeju, trying to get as much cash as possible out of him, in exchange for the shoes they had stolen earlier. What they don't know is that the jeeju has already called for the extra pair of shoes lying in his car and he's just messing with them, toying with their hopes because we all know that they ain't getting anything. This is not the set of *Hum Aapke Hain Kaun* and the jeeju is definitely not Salman Khan aka Prem. Frankly, it's been a while since I have seen any kind of excitement regarding the whole shoe stealing business. It was very popular when I was growing up, but now people are not interested in an activity that doesn't involve the bar, the dance floor or—if you're really in the mood—jumping on tables.

The friends of the bride and groom are still at the bar, far away from all the wedding mania and rona-dhona. They are waiting for the wedding ceremony to end, so that they can congratulate the couple and involve them in some much-needed fun and frolic—and of course, continue drinking.

But not so soon, you crazy geezers, *kyunki picture abhi baaki hai*. Once the Mr and Mrs part of the programme is completed, it's time to deal with approximately 2,500 people, before making it to the bar. People are literally waiting in line to congratulate the couple and get a picture clicked with them. It's sort of like the hotdog line at Disneyland, but instead of a delicious hotdog, all you get at the end of this line is a fake 'thank you' and a standard template picture. I really don't understand the purpose of this exercise. What do couples do with 2,500 pictures in the same pose, but with different people, out of which 80 per cent have no clue who you are and vice versa. But as tradition goes, what has to be done has to be done. No ifs and buts.

The silver lining to this monotonous exercise is that— oh wait, there is no silver lining. In fact, it is followed by just another tedious function (wait, *another* function? Nooo!) called the reception. Yes, we are crazy. Four hundred and fifty-two parties are not enough. We need one more.

Now, the couple is seated on a stage, where all the relatives and friends wish them a happy married life and present them with gifts. Traditionally, the main objective of the reception ceremony was to get the bride introduced to the numerous relatives and friends of the groom's family. But these days, the bride is well acquainted with most of these people, so the purpose really is to test her patience and piss her off. I am sure people bet on stuff like—how long will it be before the bride loses it and starts abusing in Hindi? How much longer can she fake-smile? And how many more times does she have to bend over and say 'thank you'?

Generally, the reception is held either immediately after the wedding (bingo—two birds with one stone) or the next day or after a few days. It is like an extension of marriage festivities, spilling beyond the main ceremony. Once again, we have elaborate entertainment, music and dance performers, and the best of the best of everything to amuse the guests (I am not going to repeat myself). Some receptions even have cultural programmes to add a dash of colour to the festive air. Unlike the wedding, the groom's parents host the reception. It's their way of welcoming the new daughter-in-law into their lives. (It also provides some solace to the bride's parents—a wedding function for which they *don't* have to pay.)

There is a last ritual that symbolizes the end of the marriage, and this is the vidaai. It's the start of a new journey for the bride, as she departs from her parents' house to go with her husband and his family. The bride's family members become extremely sentimental at this point, more because of the symbolism of the moment rather than the reality of it. It feels odd to be officially giving your daughter to another family. But the reality of the situation is that she's only moving a few blocks away, and the parents will probably see her more often after marriage than they did when she lived at home (at least in some cases). Unlike her pre-marriage days, when she lied to her parents and snuck out to meet her boyfriend, she will now lie to her husband and hang out with the parents. We girls are really messed up. The grass is always greener on the other side—well, at least, when we look through our beer goggles.

My sister is the perfect example of this change post marriage. (Sorry, sis, for using you as an example for everything, but remember, if my book is a bestseller, I am taking you to South America for a holiday.) Before marriage, she would always crib, 'Why are Mom and Dad so demanding?' 'Oh god, *now* what do they want?' 'Dude,

I can't wait to get out of here!' And now? 'I am coming over for dinner'; 'let's do lunch'; 'meet me please'; 'I love you, Mom and Dad'; 'you guys are the best!' Is it just me or am I right when I view this as hypocrisy at its best? Well, whatever it is, it seems to work, and both parties are happy.

🖎

After the vidaai, the bride and groom sit in their fancy car, decorated with flowers, and drive off into the sunset to embrace a fairy tale ending. Well, at least that's the plan. No one knows what the future has in store for them, so all one can do is stop being a pest and hope for the best!

Anyway, this is not the time to worry about matrimonial issues, as the couple has first class tickets to the much-awaited one-month-long honeymoon. I doubt anyone would have a fight in the penthouse suite at the Four Seasons, or while driving around New Zealand in a fancy sports car, or while sunbathing in Rio. A honeymoon is no longer a one-week vacation in Goa (sorry Mom and Dad, but that's just lame!). It is a semester-long, country-hopping and world-conquering adventure, with five star hotels, no cheap motels, luxury cars, and rooftop bars. The most important person on speed dial is not the doctor or lawyer, but the concierge from American Express.

It really is a dream. Being born rich is the best thing that can happen to you. Of course, you will never have the personality and confidence of the self-made man, but who cares? You have Papa to fall back on and you can pay people to look up to you. *Aur kya chahiye?* And most importantly—you've got the Dom Pérignon and VVIP passes to Tomorrowland!

Postscript

So, those who are inheriting the good stuff, go plan your next vacation. And the rest of you awesome people, please ignore everything I have said in this book, because I have just been having fun!

Love is a beautiful thing and marriage, a wonderful institution. My parents have been very happily married now for over thirty years and love each other passionately. My brother-in-law is one of the nicest people I know and I can guarantee that my sister and he, too, will have the most awesome marriage just like my parents. I am the problem child, who likes to scandalize and scar, and therefore, this book. It is definitely based on reality, but with lots of mirch, masala and tadka, just to make you laugh and forget your problems temporarily. If I manage to bring a moment of entertainment to even one person who reads this book, I will consider it a bestseller.

Epilogue

The days of sati-savitri and abla-naari are long gone, with girls becoming more confident and feisty. The men, on the other hand, haven't changed all that much. They were assholes then, and they are assholes now (with all due respect). They had double standards then, and they have double standards now. They want to date a rockstar, but marry the nun from next door. The girlfriend may look hot in a short skirt, but the wife looks hotter in a burkha. WTF? The good news is that women are now learning how to successfully deal with this species, which is very similar to coping with Rottweilers—show no fear!

I remember the year I turned twenty-one; it was great. I had graduated from college and started working in London, loving and living my life to the fullest. My grandparents, on the other hand, were getting worried, and started trying to find the perfect husband for their now-eligible granddaughter. My grandmom used to get very upset with me when I'd tell her that love and loyalty were extremely important and that I would only marry a man who was crazy about me and did not have a roving eye. She told me I was a fool and that all men would cheat. I believe, her exact words were, '*Sab aadmi moo maarte hain, aur yeh love-shove kuch nahi hota. Itne nakhre honge toh kabhi shaadi nahi hogi!*'

That was the first time in my life that I was completely speechless. I mean if this was how my granny thought, how could I expect a man to understand? Luckily, my parents supported me in my quest for loyalty and now I am thirty-one years old and still single. Sometimes, I wonder, was my granny right? Are we 'modern' girls too picky? All the qualities that we expect to find in men—do they even exist?

Well, I certainly hope so.

Acknowledgments

I would like to express my gratitude to the many people who saw me through the process of writing this book; to all those who provided support, talked things over, read, wrote, offered comments, allowed me to quote their remarks and assisted with the editing, proofreading and design.

A special and sincere thanks to my friend, father figure, philosopher, guide and guru—the legendary Suhel Seth, who helped me through every step of this journey, supported and encouraged me, and without whom there would be no book.

I would like to thank my parents for their unconditional support and for their faith in me; my sister and brother-in-law who read my manuscript a million times and gave me priceless feedback; my close friends and family who consistently encouraged me and never let me doubt myself.

A thank you to all these rockstars for accompanying me on the journey towards my dreams.